EMPTY HAND REVOLUTION
THE UNFINISHED LIFE OF COSMO ZIMIK

BASED ON A TRUE STORY

David Mark Brown

In Partnership with the Morung Project

David Mark Brown has captured the amazing and miraculous events of Cosmo's life in this exciting book. Cosmo is one among the special persons I have had the opportunity to know and work with. Highly talented, sincere and dynamic, I'm confident the Lord will use him more and more in the lives of hundreds and thousands of young people through his *Empty Hand Revolution*.

Mark Visvasam
Former Director of Athletes in Action India
Current National Representative of Kingdoms Harvest International

Empty Hand Revolution: The Unfinished Life of Cosmo Zimik
David Mark Brown

Electronic Edition Copyright © 2014 by David Mark Brown. All rights reserved.
Cover Design by Brian Loeber

No part of this publication may be reproduced, stored in a retrieval system, or transmitted in any way by any means, electronic, mechanical, photocopy, recording or otherwise without the prior permission of the author except as provided by USA copyright law.

While this book is based on a true story, events, dates, names and other details have been altered significantly enough to render it a work of fiction. Some characters, descriptions, entities, and incidents included in the story are products of the author's imagination, thus their resemblance to actual persons, events, and entities is entirely coincidental.

CreateSpace
Morung Project, 2014
Nampa, ID 83651
www.MorungProject.com
ISBN: 1495990362
First Print Edition, Copyright © 2014 by David Mark Brown. All rights reserved.
Cover Design by Brian Loeber

Published in the United States of America
Morung Project

- I. -Foreword by Frans Welman
- II. -Prologue: At the End of an AK-47

Part One: Life in the Village — 13

- Jungle Marooned, 1975
- History: The British Era
- Hawai Mangan on Christmas Eve
- History: The Struggle for Independence
- Bringing Home Snakes
- History: The God of Nagalim
- Village School Days
- Surviving Village Life

Part Two: Manhood in Manipur — 43

- Respect and Intimidation
- Training a Warrior
- Note to Reader: Blank Pages Ahead
- At the End of an AK-47, Take Two
- Healing Never Comes Easy
- History: Oinam and Operation Bluebird
- I've Been Expecting You
- The Prodigal Meets King David
- History: Development of the Naga Worldview

Part Three: A New Chapter in Delhi — 75

- Run-in With a Rickshaw
- Naga Party Life
- Introducing the Girl
- The Lure of the Fight
- Delhi Fight Club
- Fight Culture and Opportunity
- Conflicts of Interest
- Culture: Politics and the Dalits
- A Meeting in the Jungle
- A Home Without Snakes
- A Father's Warning
- A Rainy Day
- Entrepreneurialism
- Battlefield
- The Devil Collects Twice

Part Four: Second Chances   126

- Stranded and Alone
- The Bad News
- A Stranger in The Gym
- Getting a Job
- Herding Goats
- They Came for a Show
- Kung Fu for Jesus
- Teaching in the Temple
- Battlefield, Part Two
- Kumar Returns

Part Five: Loose Cannons   163

- Parting Ways With AIA
- Another Author's Note
- Leaps and Bounds
- The Big Event
- Church Partners
- I'll Burn You Down
- Grasping Hands

Part Six: Out of India   191

- Trip to Thailand
- Introducing the New Girl
- Hong Kong Courtship
- Meeting the Family
- Meeting the Family, Part Two
- Bumpy Spell
- Idaho Calm
- Idaho Desert

Epilogue: In Cosmo's Own Words   225

- The View From Nampa, Idaho
- The Morung Project
- Welcome to the Empty Hand Revolution
- III. ~A Greeting from the Author
- IV. ~Appendices

FOREWORD

Cosmo Zimik is one of thousands of young lads and young ladies from the forest of Naga Nation, currently divided between India and Myanmar, who has endured manifold ordeals. Although neither country could show they 'owned' the Naga Nation when the British decided to vacate their colony, the international community acknowledged the Naga Nation as part of both countries. The effects of this neglect by the then British Government (1947) have devastated the lives of thousands of Nagas like Cosmo Zimik.

Thus, the story of Cosmo is an important one, not because of him, but because he is the prime example of a Naga who has been a victim of oppression, suppression, persecution, torture and more. This only because the Naga peoples took their right to self determination seriously; seriously enough to properly defend it for over sixty years.

Cosmo escaped the turmoil in his region to land in Delhi, the capital of India and so the lion's den. Like so many before and after him, he learned how to be effective. By being effective, I do not mean only as a missionary reaching out to others of any religious affiliation. He wanted to be effective so his people and others like the Dalits could restore or gain self-respect.

Now, Cosmo desires to set another example; this time for his own people and the development they need to properly, and in a dignified manner, sustain themselves. Aside from the atrocities committed by the Indian Army, Cosmo wants to contribute to the cultural resilience of the Nagas and is starting with one of their smallest tribes: the Tarao.

I cannot claim to have known Cosmo a long time, but I do know he is inspired. Perhaps not in the political sense of the word by way of joining the armed and rather divided movement for independence, but certainly in the humanistic sense of the word.

Cosmo is inspired to uplift the standard of living of the Nagas to a self-sustaining level. This is something the Naga were before the alien British, Indians and Burmese claimed Naga lands as their own. After all, Nagas were never conquered, and so history shows they were never defeated.

Cosmo, I hope, will inspire the forty or more Naga tribes (and all of us) to live an honorable life—a life of peace and respect for each other and our neighbors. So, in spite of differences we face, I recommend this book to anyone with a heart for justice and identity. I recommend it for anyone who opposes racism and oppression.

Frans Welman
Naga International Support Center
Author of *Forbidden Land – The Quest for Nagalim*
and *Beyond Twilight*.

EMPTY HAND REVOLUTION
THE UNFINISHED LIFE OF COSMO ZIMIK

"A small body of determined spirits
fired by an unquenchable faith in their mission
can alter the course of history."
Mahatma Gandhi

"Each of us has an impossible lesson to teach the world.
In most cases, these are false lessons
the world has taught us."
David Mark Brown

PROLOGUE:

At the End of an AK-47

Manipur State, 1989

COSMO OPENED HIS EYES at the slightest sound approaching him from behind. His senses quickly gathered how long he'd been meditating. The sky remained dark. The jungle had reached its quietest point during day or night. Dew had settled on his arms and legs. Within minutes, the first tinges of pink, orange and yellow would crest over the horizon like the ripe skin of a mango.

"How close did I make it before you heard me this time?" Damu spoke in a whisper.

"Fifteen meters." Cosmo drew a deep breath.

"Between meditation and fighting, I don't know how you have time for studies." Damu sat beside his friend without stirring the silence of the early morning jungle.

"I only study what's important."

"I thought the teachers decided that."

"To the teacher everything is important. That makes nothing important." Cosmo had yet to move anything except his eyes and mouth.

"Profound. Is that the kind of crap you come up with out here in the jungle?"

Losing discipline, Cosmo punched his friend in the shoulder.

Then they both sat still for several minutes.

"It's quiet. You don't get that in the city, or on the lake." Damu paused, as if tasting the silence. "When I was a boy, the fishermen worked day and night. The surface of Loktak Lake never rested. Then the government released the carp. They dumped them by the millions. Combine invasive species with pollution and fertilizers, and the lake is dying. There's nothing for the Manipuri to do but drink or fight."

The silence between the two friends thickened.

Damu sighed. "Sometimes I wonder if I've chosen correctly."

Cosmo slapped his thighs and jumped up like an uncoiling viper. "To drink is to surrender. The Manipuri's only mistake is that they fight each other."

Damu leapt to his feet. "You would have us fight the Assam Rifles? A street gang against an army of Jawans? You know better than anyone what they did at Oinam."

Cosmo gripped his friend's shoulders. "You think too small. Haven't we trained our new recruits? Haven't we grown larger and stronger than ever? Haven't we become disciplined? Where you see quibbling street gangs, I see an army waiting for the right leader."

Damu scoffed. "I suppose you imagine yourself as that leader? You forget your place."

Cosmo shook his head. "No, I am not Manipuri. You are. These are your people."

Damu sucked air through his teeth. "The other gangs would never listen to me."

"Respect." Cosmo wielded the word like a sword. "Three years ago you told me you hungered for it. Together, we could demand it."

"Shhh." Damu turned his ear toward the creeping sunrise. "Did you hear that?"

The teens froze for several seconds. After hearing nothing, Cosmo suspected Damu had stooped to fakery to change the subject.

"I guess it was nothing." Damu breathed deeply. "You ready to head back? Imphal City is bound to have missed us by now."

Cosmo sighed. "I should visit my parents first."

"Feeling guilty, huh?"

"My mother misses me, and there's only my sisters at home now."

Damu stretched. "Suit yourself. You'll never make it back before session starts."

"My father is pastoring a church in Marao. If I take the bus, I'll make it."

"Good luck. I'll be thinking of you this afternoon as I'm reclining in the shade at Kangla Park."

Cosmo lunged at Damu lazily.

Damu blocked the effort. The two friends sparred half-heartedly for a few seconds.

Cosmo held up his hands, breaking off the friendly combat before it got serious. "We'll call it a draw."

Damu laughed. "I guess I'll see you Monday." Nimbly, and in total darkness, he set out in a westerly direction. "May the jungle conceal your presence."

"And you as well." Cosmo closed his eyes. He listened to Damu's footfalls fade. Minutes later, he flinched and opened his eyes. Without his knowing, the peace of the jungle had entranced him—until something had broken the trance.

An uneasy feeling hung over him as he jogged toward the village where he and Damu had spent the night. Normally, Cosmo would have packed his belt, canteen and gi inside his rolled up bamboo mat and slung the whole thing over his shoulder before leaving the community center. But Damu had been sleeping, and Cosmo hadn't wanted to wake him.

By the time he reached the outskirts of the village, the mosquito buzz in the distance had grown into the unmistakable growl of a motorcade—a caravan of Jeeps. In the dim light of predawn, Cosmo sprinted toward the community center in the middle of the village. Smoke rose from chimneys, as the flicker of cook fires danced inside darkened windows.

Cosmo's first impulse was to warn the villagers. But he couldn't be certain of who played the cat, or who played the mouse. His mind raced faster than his body. The Jeeps showing up this morning couldn't be a coincidence. Someone had given him and Damu up.

Cosmo swore under his breath and kept running, the community center within a hundred meters. Cosmo's possessions were meager. He couldn't afford to leave anything behind, especially not his belt and gi.

He just had to get his stuff and clear the edge of the village. In the jungle, in the dark, no one would find him. But the growl of engines grew too quickly.

Roads in Nagalim, where Cosmo had grown up, were intentionally serpentine—constructed as early detection systems during decades of constant conflict with India's Central Government. In Manipur, many of the roads were built for convenience, without considering whose convenience they'd serve.

By the time Cosmo reached the community center, dancing Jeep headlights were visible through the jungle canopy on the edge of the village. Without slowing down, Cosmo kicked in the paneled door of the community center, splintering it and knocking it from its bottom hinges.

He skidded to a stop and scoured the dark for his things. They weren't where he'd left them. Something didn't feel right. He stretched his ears for any indication of human presence. What he heard was the release of the charging handle of an AK-47 as it chambered a 39mm cartridge.

PART 1

LIFE IN THE VILLAGE

Jungle Marooned, 1975

NOTHING ABOUT THE SURROUNDINGS was alien except the mood. The tangy spice of decomposing cardamom pods intermingled with the odor of Cosmo's own sweat. The bracken of the jungle floor, the high-pitched call of warblers, the distant chattering of the river from the base of the valley—these were the telltale signs of home. The fear and the cowering—those were alien.

A branch snapped nearby. A curious troop of Rhesus monkeys skittered upward into the tender, green branches of the jungle ceiling. Their shifting movements cast ephemeral beams of noonday light onto the jungle floor. The glinting rays revealed the presence of smoke filtering uphill. The acrid scent of burning thatch tickled the hairs in Cosmo's nose.

He pushed further out from under the smothering embrace of his mother. The skin around her right eye had begun to swell and change from the color of chocolate to a bruised sunset. Despite her silent rebuke, Cosmo struggled to free himself like a snake shedding his skin.

The rustling of leaves some meters off focused his attention. He felt the eyes of a few dozen villagers doing the same. Surely militants could not travel so quietly through the jungle. Why was no one revealing themselves? Why were they not greeting the person who must be one of their own?

Cosmo gasped as his oldest brother, Aring, emerged into a small clearing beneath a banyan tree. The only one of the villagers to move, Cosmo burst from his mother's grip. He lunged toward Aring but stopped short of embracing him.

The two boys locked eyes. Swollen and cut, Aring's forehead and cheeks were smeared with blood, mud and bracken. The jungle paused for breath as tectonic plates shifted in a small boy's reality.

Despite having barely reached his fourth year, Cosmo knew this moment changed everything. Had it not been for Aring, he would have been beaten by the soldiers—generic commandos to a boy taught to run rather than identify his attackers.

This morning there hadn't been time to run. The soldiers had parked their Jeeps out of earshot and hiked over the hill. They'd streamed into the village like ants beneath the cover of cut leaves.

Cosmo knew the bruises up and down Aring's bloodied body would have been aimed at himself and their mother. Cosmo's eyes swelled. Certainly their mother would have sustained much worse than fists and the butt of an AK-47. Instead, his older brother had taken it all, allowing Cosmo and the others to escape.

Gunshots echoed from their village at the bottom of the valley. Cosmo jerked from his trance. Aring blinked, his eyes drifting out of focus. Swaying on his feet and dripping with blood, he maintained his defiance.

To Cosmo, his brother's face had been chiseled from solid rock and etched with courage—half monument, half man.

Slow and steady, Aring raised his arm and placed it around Cosmo's shoulder. At this, their mother leapt to her feet and embraced them both. Even as the Rhesus monkeys returned to their lower perches for a better view, the rest of the villagers remained hidden by the jungle.

Days after the attack, the people of Cosmo's village remained in the jungle. As long as the embers continued to smoke, the people waited. Their meager possessions had been burned, much of the village razed to the ground for no other reason than intimidation.

A generation earlier, the village defenses would have included a trench and a bamboo wall. More of the warrior-aged men would have been nearby rather than scattered abroad to earn a living. Two generations earlier, their only enemies had been other Nagas and the neighboring Kukis, a people who had long lived among the Naga. Three generations ago, the Naga had been proud warriors who treasured the heads of fallen enemies, stockpiling them in the Morung at the center of the village.

For better or for worse, all of that had changed by the 1970's when Cosmo had been born into a second-generation Christian family determined to raise their children under the peaceful banner of God. Unfortunately, peace would remain hard to come by in Nagalim (Land of the Naga).

After the embers cooled, some of the villagers rebuilt. Others, including Cosmo, his mother and his siblings, continued to live in the wild. They gathered corn, potatoes, rice and ghost chilies from the fields the soldiers had spared or failed to notice. They rounded up pigs that had scattered during the raid.

They shared with neighbors. They borrowed from the land. Even encroachment from the outside world had not alienated the Naga from the jungle. Soldiers could burn their village, but their jungle home would always remain.

When Cosmo's father returned from his preaching circuit among neighboring villages, his family finally rebuilt. But for Cosmo, the fires the soldiers lit would burn throughout much of his life in the form of anger, guilt and regret.

He wished he would have helped—that he would have been brave like his oldest brother. The need to become a warrior, for himself and for his people, ignited furiously inside him. The Naga's struggle for self-determination had hatched in his heart during the first of many moments that would threaten to either consume him or shape him into something great.

History: The British Era

THE NAGA INHABIT A remote and mountainous section of jungle straddling the border of northeast India and Burma (Myanmar). Until British efforts to incorporate Naga lands in the late nineteenth century, the Naga peoples quarreled only among themselves and neighboring Kukis.

Due to the ruggedness of the land and the stiff resistance of the Nagas, the British aborted their efforts after controlling only a small section of what they labeled the Naga Hills. The Nagas' hard earned rest didn't last.

During World War II, the British called on Nagas, their former rivals, to help repel the Japanese who sought to establish a land route into India. Determined to preserve their land from all invaders, Naga warriors responded overwhelmingly. As a result, they played a decisive role in driving the Japanese out during the critical Battle of Kohima, frequently referred to as the "Stalingrad of the East."

For their assistance, the Naga earned a bit of proper respect from the British. Unfortunately, that respect never produced a payoff.

After the war, as the British packed up their bags to officially vacate the Indian subcontinent, they failed to leave decisive instructions behind in regards to the hazy region between Burma, China, Bhutan, Bangladesh and the infant Republic of India. This disputed territory included the Naga Hills.

Mahatma Gandhi famously opined that the Naga should be granted the right to self governance if they so desired it, just as the people of India desired it from the British: "Nagas have every right to be independent. We did not want to live under the domination of the British and they are now leaving us."

When questioned further about Indian threats of violence in the disputed region, Gandhi continued, "I will come to the Naga Hills. I will ask them to shoot me first before one Naga is shot." Unfortunately, Gandhi didn't live long enough to follow through with this promise.

Indeed, it had never been and would never be in doubt that Nagas wanted nothing else than to be left alone.

But the newly forming Republic of India incorporated dozens of distinct and geographically concentrated ethnic groups. It didn't take long for the young republic, led by Prime Minister Jawaharlal Nehru, to demonstrate its panic over the possibility of those groups forming independent nations.

To make the matter more confusing, the British had never fully occupied Nagalim, or the area they referred to as the Naga Hills. As far as most of the remote Nagas were concerned, they had always been and remained independent. How could the British hand them over to India, if the British had never conquered them to begin with?

One day before India declared their independence on August 15th, 1947, Nagalim declared its own. By 1956, India and the Naga were engaged in a bloody war that spanned the majority of four decades, and still to this day has yet to be resolved.

Hawai Mangan on Christmas Eve

"HERE, GIVE THIS ONE to your brother." Cosmo's mother ushered him out of the bamboo hut with two delicately wrapped bundles. Cosmo stood quietly for several seconds, staring at the packages, one in each hand.

His mother's version of hawai mangan wasn't a perfect replica of the treat his friends were already buying at the fair. Instead of newspaper, the snacks were packaged in sheets of used notebook paper and bound with fine strands of bamboo. Still, they were wonderful.

Cosmo held a package up to his nose. The garlic, ghost chili and beans fried in oil made his eyes and mouth water. His mother had done an amazing job. These homemade hawai mangan would outdo any from the vendors.

After tucking the precious cargo into his hand-me-down jacket, Cosmo ran to catch up with his older brother, Ramrei. The nearest to him in age, Ramrei was most often Cosmo's cohort in crime. Today, the two of them were on their way to the village fair held every year on Christmas Eve.

The rest of their siblings, Aton, Vasty, Atip, Aring and Rock, had been dismissed early to attend. Cosmo and Ramrei had been asked to stay back and finish chores.

The extra work had been a small ransom in exchange for not attending the fair empty handed. Ramrei had more than grumbled until Cosmo had volunteered to finish all of the female chores, leaving his older brother with nothing but chopping wood.

To Cosmo, work was work, whether it was cleaning, carrying water or tilling the earth. Why so much fuss? He actually enjoyed the opportunity to lighten his mother's burden.

The thought of his mother constantly slaving to keep the family fed panged him with guilt—some of which he deserved. While carrying water had saved his mother from a portion of her backbreaking labor, his whining had resulted in her spending much of the morning preparing hawai mangan.

Cosmo's step hitched as his flip-flop came undone. Stooping, he threaded the plastic toe divider back through the rubber sole. The fit was getting loose. He'd have to be more conscious of gripping the bottom with his toes. The thought depressed him enough to need another whiff of the hawai mangan. Sneaking a bundle from his jacket, he held it beneath his nose. *Heavenly.*

Tucking the prize safely away, Cosmo doubled his pace. On this most important day of the year, many of the village children would indulge in more than fried bean treats. Hawai mangan was the required minimum. Without it, the fair could hardly be considered complete.

For everyone else, the spicy snacks would be purchased from vendors for the cost of a single rupee. Unfortunately, that was a rupee more than Cosmo's parents could afford. *No one will ever know the difference.* Cosmo reassured himself as he hurried toward the football field in the center of town.

Families increasingly clogged the main road. Children emerged from their homes. Some were already returning, perhaps to escort younger siblings.

The popular music had been blaring from the center of the village loud enough for Cosmo to hear traces of it even inside his home. Now he recognized an American pop song by the Bee Gees, one of the musical groups his brother had exposed him to.

Cosmo hoped he hadn't missed his favorite game of kabaddi. Usually the early hours of the fair were spent alternating between tug of war and pole climbing—neither of which Cosmo excelled at. Kabaddi was different.

While the bigger kids were stronger than Cosmo, he could attack with quick bursts of power and agility. His ability to escape back to his team's side of the field without being caught made him an ideal raider. He was never the first chosen for a match. More importantly, he was never the last.

With his stomach rumbling and his flip-flop clenched between his toes, Cosmo finally caught up to his brother. The music had switched to one of his favorite Indian hits, Sholay Sholay. The song's beat captured him. Not knowing more than five words in Hindi, he hadn't the slightest idea what the song was about.

"About time," Ramrei said. "Do you have them?"

Cosmo grinned while catching his breath.

"This better work." Ramrei didn't seem as enthusiastic about their mother's plan.

"Wait until you see them."

Surrounded by dozens of other children from their own clan, the boys finished their stroll to the center of the village without another word. They altered their route slightly to ensure they'd remain among their own. Just in case. Most likely none of the tougher kids from other clans would start trouble on the day of the fair. But in the village, cautious behavior became ingrained behavior.

As the boys reached the fringes of the fair, Ramrei took Cosmo by the sleeve and pulled him behind the community center. "Okay, give me mine."

Still grinning, Cosmo carefully removed one of the packages and held it out to his brother.

Shaking his head, Ramrei took it.

"What?"

"Notebook paper?"

"So?"

"Nothing. It doesn't matter."

"What is it?" Cosmo demanded.

Ramrei brushed him off. "I'll meet you for the kabaddi match, okay? Go check on our sisters."

Cosmo nodded, but his grin had dissolved. As he watched his

brother stride away, he wondered about the fried bean snacks their mother had spent all morning making for them. The wrapping couldn't make that much difference. He shrugged. Ramrei was only being morose. It wouldn't be the first time.

Cosmo ran to the crowded fair entrance and waited to be admitted. He stood on tiptoes. Now all he had to do was locate his friends and show them he had been able to purchase snacks like everyone else. He'd check on his sisters after that. Besides, his father had probably found them already.

As he passed through the entrance, he grew dizzy on the smells of hawai mangan and other fried treats, both sweet and spicy. Cardamom, curry, ginger, garlic—the smells wafted over the crowd. Cosmo pushed further into the heart of the fair.

Passing several vendors, his mouth began to water. His stomach gnawed at itself with hunger. He wondered if he could hold out until he found his friends. With the wrapped snacks clutched in his hand, he thought he could taste them already.

Finally, Cosmo found a clump of his classmates. He sidled up next to Samuel, a pudgy child who shared Cosmo's burden of intelligence but lacked Cosmo's ambition. With a flourish, Cosmo presented his bundle of fried treats. Not wanting his friends to focus on the wrapping, he quickly tore into it. "I've got the best hawai mangan in the whole fair."

As Cosmo watched his friends' dubious faces in response to his boast, he understood the disappointment his brother had expressed earlier. Despite his friends' doubt, Cosmo continued to display the snacks proudly in the palm of his hand.

"How come it doesn't look the same as everyone else's?"

"Where did you get it?"

"What is that? Used notebook paper?" Samuel tried to poke it with a finger.

"Oh, that." Quick to improvise, Cosmo laughed. "This is premium. Very special. I bought it from a vendor who made only a small batch. This was the last one!"

Unconvinced, the children scrutinized the wrapping and the

snack from different angles. "What makes it so special?"

Samuel shook his head and attempted to assert himself as the leader of the pack, despite a status barely higher than Cosmo's. "It doesn't look that different."

Cosmo winked. "Here, just a little taste for each of you. Then you'll understand." He offered the other children tiny pieces. As they sampled his mother's hawai mangan, his plan bloomed into full fruition.

"I see!"

"It's wonderful." Samuel exclaimed. Forgetting his earlier resistance, he reached for more.

Cosmo smacked Samuel's hand. On the outside he remained smug, even victorious. On the inside, his heart sank into his stomach. Everyone in the village could afford to buy their snacks on the most important day of the year. Everyone except him and his brother, who couldn't scrounge up two rupees between them.

It angered him that his mother had been forced to work so hard to maintain the lie. It shamed him that he had clung to her so tightly, begging her not to send him to the festival empty-handed. It shamed him further that maintaining the deception remained so important.

Cosmo determined to do something about it, but what? As bitter as they were spicy, Cosmo ate his bean snack wearing a phony grin. His stomach rumbled as he finished. The heat baked into most of his mother's cooking helped mask the hunger. But he longed for more than chilies. This moment merely added to the long list of moments that fueled his ambition to rise above village life. He and all Nagas deserved more.

Eventually, he stared down at his empty hands. An opportunity would arise. He would know it when he saw it—the chance to never worry about empty hands or empty pockets, or an empty stomach again.

Until then, he would keep grinning.

History: The Struggle for Independence

DURING ITS EARLY YEARS, the war between the new Republic of India and the Naga took on all the hallmarks of a guerilla conflict. After a series of escalating events, the Indian army poured 100,000 troops into the isolated and rugged Nagalim in 1956. They assumed their overwhelming forces would subdue the Naga fighters, and thus end the conflict in a matter of weeks or possibly months.

The Nagas disagreed with the Indian assessment. With the help of the Naga National Council (NNC), the loosely knit Naga tribes rallied together with surprising speed and efficiency during the years after declaring independence in 1947. By 1956, they had formed the Federal Government of Nagaland and the Naga Home Guard. Soon after India launched their first major offensive, the Naga began countering with guerilla tactics.

It turned out the British had taught the Naga a handful of valuable lessons. One of those lessons had been that people outside of Nagalim have unexplainable ambitions to acquire lands not their own. Some Nagas had traveled broadly during WWII while fighting for the Allied forces. They had seen enough to understand the outside world would not leave them alone without a fight.

When India came in force, enough Nagas were ready. They plunged into the jungle and invited the inexperienced Indian conscripts to come after them. Naga fighters routinely raided arms caches. They made a practice of stripping captured Indian soldiers of their weapons and gear just to send them home. This behavior insulted the

Indian government further.

Accustomed to a style of tribal combat between neighbors and distant relatives, the slaughtering of their foe made little sense to Nagas. Contrary to popular belief, their headhunting ancestors had removed the heads of fallen enemies to demonstrate prowess as well as respect. The soul, or center, of a human resided in the head. To Nagas, taking human life indiscriminately and disrespecting the bodies afterward, according to the manner observed in WWII, seemed barbaric.

As the violence increased, Indian forces frequently abandoned their attempts to confront Naga guerillas directly. Instead they attacked and burned villages. To assist in the legality of these practices, the dreaded Armed Forces Special Powers Act (based on a British ordinance from 1942) was passed by the Parliament of India in 1958. The act essentially granted any and all military personal within designated "disturbed areas" the right to do whatever they deemed necessary to regain the peace without fear of legal reprisal.

As a result, a relentless string of unspeakable atrocities scarred Nagalim for a decade. Incensed and insulted by the ferocity of Naga resistance, Indian officers ordered the rape and murder of women and children. They burned villages repeatedly. Many Nagas claim not a single village survived the 50's and 60's without being burned at least once. Some villages, like Khonoma, were reportedly burned several times.

Since most of the people with firsthand experience of these atrocities have already died, it's likely the larger world will never know the exact details of these dark times.

In 1964, a ceasefire was signed between the Naga National Council and the Government of India. During the two years that followed, it appeared a resolution might be possible. But ultimately, the Naga broke off the talks when the Indian offerings fell short of total autonomy.

Depending on who is asked, opinions on the ceasefire vary widely. Some say the ceasefire was never genuinely honored. Some say it broke off in 1967 with the end of the peace talks. Others insist it still continues today.

While the violence never again reached the same terrible degree and scale as during the late 50's and early 60's, it is certain the violence did not end. Neither did the Naga's unyielding resolve. The caste system of India could not accommodate their comparatively egalitarian society. They had no other home. Thus they chose to fight for self-determination and autonomy until the death.

Bringing Home Snakes

"THIS WAY. I THINK I saw something." Cosmo leapt a small tributary of the main river before crouching atop its steep bank.

Ramrei followed behind him. "Why are we bothering with this? Snake meat is horrible. We might as well go spider hunting."

Cosmo brushed aside a clump of scrub oak, an invasive species that multiplied behind his back. "There, in the sand. I see one."

"Or steal scraps from high town."

Cosmo shook his head and hissed. "You're wrong. A Kuki boy from Pashong told me snake tastes like monkey, or even dog. We can take these home. Mother will cook them."

Ramrei rolled his eyes. "Mother hates snakes."

"How do you know?" Cosmo remained firm.

"Fine, we'll kill some snakes. But you're the one taking them home."

Cosmo faced the river. Its waters were receded. In a month's time, after the rains began, the rocky embankment where they crouched would be under water. Below the two boys, a glistening black snake uncoiled and slithered toward a hole in the muddy bank. "It's getting away. I'll grab the tail, you smash the head."

Without waiting for a response, Cosmo jumped the two meters from the bank to the sandbar. His bare feet sank into the wet sand.

Ramrei strode further along the bank before springing down to join his younger brother. The yellow and black banded snake didn't flinch at the boys' presence, its head already disappeared down the hole.

"No you don't." Cosmo snatched the flickering tail, yanked the snake backward and let go. What had appeared a meter-long snake now looked closer to two meters long.

"A big boy." Ramrei whistled through his teeth. He held a bamboo stick in one hand and a rock the size of a monkey skull in the other.

Exposed, the snake quickly coiled into a knot.

Ramrei clucked his tongue and nodded toward Cosmo. "One more time."

Gripping the tail a second time, Cosmo dragged the snake into a straight line.

"Gotcha." Ramrei struck with a swift whack of his stick, pinning the snake behind the head. A second later he brought the rock smashing down, but with less than the desired effect. "The sand is too soft!"

The body of the snake jolted and writhed.

"Hold down the head." Cosmo released the tail and rushed to his brother's side. Using the bamboo stick like a spear, he stabbed at the writhing snake. His first shot deflected off the slippery hide and sank into the sand.

"Hurry, before he gets loose." Ramrei held the rock in place, his hands dangerously close to the angry snake's buried head.

Cosmo stood on the snake with both feet, clamping its rubbery skin between his toes. He took a deep breath and aimed the sharp end of the bamboo stick. With a precise stab, he pierced the snake. Simultaneously, both boys jumped clear and watched the animal's final throes.

"Next time you take the head." Ramrei slapped Cosmo on the back and both boys laughed.

Cosmo tugged the bamboo stick from the sandbar and tossed it up onto the embankment, snake and all. "Maybe the next one should be smaller."

Using scrub oak for handholds, the boys scrambled up the slope. Ramrei crushed the snake's head with a second blow from his rock for good measure.

Cosmo removed the stick and hung the snake in the low saddle of a nearby oak tree. "Two more?"

Ramrei nodded and the boys continued their hunt. On their left the river ran slowly downhill and away from their village. On all sides, the jungle lured them with promises of treasure. Currently, Cosmo only cared about the ones he could eat.

An hour later, the brothers returned to the oak with three smaller snakes in addition to the large one. Cosmo slung the two-meter-long serpent over his shoulder so it wouldn't drag the ground. "Tonight we feast on snake meat!"

"What is it with you and meat?" Ramrei leapt over the tributary and continued toward the village.

"Man was meant to eat meat, not beans and vegetables." Cosmo stuck out his tongue.

"Then why is meat so expensive and vegetables so cheap?"

Cosmo shrugged. "The good things in life are always expensive."

Ramrei scoffed. "Too bad for us."

Cosmo kept his mouth shut. He didn't want to ruin a successful afternoon with bitter words. But it was too late to silence the bitter thoughts. He would get the money someday—enough money to eat meat two times a day. And not snake or monkey. He'd eat chicken and pork. He licked his lips. Especially pork.

Not wanting to draw too much attention, the boys chose a quiet path from the edge of the village to their house. Ramrei didn't seem concerned, but Cosmo was convinced if anyone noticed their prize of snake meat, they'd have to fight for it.

Having gotten ahead of his brother, Cosmo stepped off the road and scanned the branches of a plum tree while waiting for Ramrei to catch up. The buds had broken, forming tiny fruits. It'd be two months before the fruit ripened—five weeks until they became even slightly edible. Cosmo's stomach rumbled.

Finally, Ramrei shuffled past.

Cosmo joined his older brother. "Mother will be so happy." He dangled the smaller snakes in his hand. "I can't wait until she sees them."

"Me neither." Ramrei continued his unhurried stride.

The boys returned home without event, and Cosmo burst through the bamboo door with the snakes dangling from his outstretched arms. No one greeted him. "Mother?" He faced Ramrei. "She should be cooking by now."

Ramrei pointed with his chin. "Fire's going. Maybe she's in the garden."

Cosmo grunted. "This one's getting heavy." He flopped the largest snake from his shoulder and onto the table. He kept the smaller three, one in one hand, and two in the other. "Let's go find her."

Ramrei shrugged, a strange smile on his face. "Lead the way, brother."

Cosmo trotted out the door and headed for the garden in the back. A scream from inside the house stopped him short. "Mother?" He retraced his steps and shoved open the door. Trembling with excitement, Cosmo hoped to share the exultant moment with his mother.

At the sound of the door, she flinched and spun to face him.

Cosmo threw up his arms in victory, the smaller snakes still dangling from his grip, and approached her with his gift.

Terror rippled across his mother's face. She screamed again. And again.

Cosmo frowned. Lowering his arms, he tried to offer comfort.

Dancing backward, she screamed even louder before bolting from the house.

"Mother?" Cosmo dropped his shoulders and froze in confusion.

"We'll have snake meat tonight!" Ramrei barely got the words out before choking on his own laughter.

In disgust, Cosmo slung the smaller snakes onto the table next to the big one and wiped his hands on his shirt.

Later that evening, after being punished by their father, the boys learned the largest of the snakes had been a banded krait, a poisonous viper. It wasn't the last time the boys hunted for snake meat. It was the last time they brought home their kill.

History: The God of Nagalim

POSSIBLY THE LARGEST INFLUENCE the British had on the Naga came in the form of Christian missionaries. From 1872 to 1954, the Naga Hills were extensively proselytized by the American Baptists.

In the history of global missions, the Baptists' mission to the Naga ranks at the very top in regards to its statistical exhaustiveness. By 1954, when all foreign missionaries were expelled from the country by the Indian government, it was estimated that nearly half the 500,000 Nagas were Christians.

In the twenty-first century, an Indian Census placed the percentage of Nagaland, one of the main three Indian states occupied by the Naga, at 90% Christian. With somewhere in the neighborhood of 1,500,000 to 2,000,000 Nagas residing in the broader area of Nagalim, the result is the densest population of Christians in India. (And the densest population of Baptists in the world.)

It is believed Rev. Miles Bronson was the first to visit the Naga in 1841, but he stayed for only a short while. Edwin W. Clark is thought to be the first missionary to serve his mission in the Naga Hills. He established the first Baptist church at Molungkimong in 1872.

Other missionaries soon followed. While the work sputtered at first, within fifty years the gospel of Jesus the Christ flourished. In 1896, William Pettigrew and his wife, Alice, became the first missionaries to work out of the area currently labeled as the Indian state of Manipur.

While one account claims the Pettigrews spent seven years without a single convert, another story records a great success. As the success story goes, Pettigrew encountered a tribal chief whose great grandfather had passed down stories of a dream about the coming of a white missionary. Due to the dream, the chief allowed the Pettigrews to live among them. Eventually the chief converted, bringing the whole Tangkhul tribe of the Naga with him.

During the twenty-first century, traditional animist beliefs have resurged throughout much of Nagalim along with the desire to preserve indigenous culture. At the same time, there has been a flourish of modern Christian revivals driven by indigenous missionaries and pastors. The first of these began in the 1970's as a generation of Naga pastors rose up to fill the void left by the exit of foreign missionaries.

Many of these indigenous pastors became well known within their circuits as powerful healers and miracle workers as well as evangelists. This was the case with Cosmo's father, Pastor Mayarbing. During the twenty-first century, unification efforts among the divided Naga tribes and regions (especially the Nagaland Nagas, the Manipur Nagas and the Burmese Nagas) have been spearheaded by local Christian communities.

As is common among oppressed peoples, the Naga have found nominal religious beliefs difficult to maintain. Instead they have turned wholeheartedly to the spiritual realm for strength. In the case of the Naga, the majority belief remains Christianity.

Village School Days

COSMO SHOT UP HIS hand. He knew the answer to the simple mathematical equation instantly.

Standing at the chalkboard, the instructor hesitated. He gazed around the room, avoiding eye contact with Cosmo for several seconds. When no other hands raised, he relented. "Cosmo."

Cosmo answered in English. "Thirty-eight minutes. That's how long it would take to walk from here to the river at an average of five kilometers an hour."

The instructor had been nodding the entire time Cosmo spoke. Normally, he would follow up an answer such as this with a request for explanation. But he had tired of feeling like a private tutor for a classroom of one. "Correct. Very good. Let's try something else. How about some English."

Groans rose from several students in the overcrowded classroom of the Oasis Primary School. Cosmo didn't mind at all. Not only had he mastered mathematics and geography by third grade, he was easily the best in his class in English and Manipuri.

He scrounged beneath his seat until he located his English vocabulary book—a loosely bound collection of advertisements and newspaper clippings in the English language.

The teacher continued. "Take out your vocabulary, everyone. I need to hear from those of you who have yet to speak up."

More groans. This time, Cosmo joined them. At eight years old, he had mastered more learning than any other child in his primary school, and probably more than half of the kids in his brother's secondary school. Often the instructor couldn't keep up.

Cosmo needed more opportunity, but his parents couldn't afford it. At the end of this term he would graduate Oasis Primary. While he would be able to learn more in his brother's secondary school, he yearned to stretch his horizons.

As the teacher called on the slower students to recite the sentences written on the board, Cosmo studied the layers of thatch overhead. He unfocused his eyes and combed the blurry patterns for new images. He challenged his mind to see past the scenes he already knew lurked there, buried in the thatch roof—a tiger, a bus, a jagged mountain side.

Eventually, Cosmo's mind wandered to the matter of boarding school. He ran the old arguments through his head, and constructed a plan to broach the matter again with his father that evening.

None of the hurdles had changed, the critical one being money. A month's worth of preaching and healing in the nearby village of Marao earned his father less than a thousand rupees. His mother had to sell rice, vegetables and ghost chilies in Litan, a dozen kilometers away, to supplement the wage.

Cosmo's shoulders sagged at the thought of his mother hauling multiple bags of rice, each weighing more than her. After all their work, his parents' combined salary barely covered basic expenses. And his father often complained about the crumbling of village solidarity, pointing out how the welfare of the poor had become overlooked.

If anyone seemed to blame, Cosmo thought it should be God. How could God care so little about his own servants and their families? He didn't even provide them with enough to eat.

Absently, Cosmo followed the lesson by drifting from the thatch to the board to his notebook. Somehow, there had to be money enough to pay for private boarding school in Manipur. Maybe not this year, but soon.

"Cosmo?"

"Huh?" He focused on the instructor.

Samuel snickered from the desk beside him.

The instructor shook his head. "Would you like to read?"

"Oh." Cosmo skimmed the advertisement the others had opened in their laps until he was fairly certain of the place where the class had left off. "For the low cost of two hundred rupees, travel between Delhi and Assam is now easier than ever. You have enjoyed our world-class tea. Now tour the beautiful countryside where the tea leaves are grown."

"Very good. That's enough. Next."

Samuel picked up where Cosmo left off, and the class moved on with their lesson.

Cosmo's mind stuck on the idea of travel beyond his village and the surrounding jungle-covered mountains. Assam lay only 400 kilometers to the northwest, yet it might as well be a world away.

On the surface, it angered him that the Indians were inviting English speakers to tour Assam. Yet, those same tourists were prevented from traveling into the restricted Naga regions like the one in which Cosmo lived. Outsiders were permitted to know about northeast India's tea, but not its people.

As he dug deeper into his thoughts, he realized the only way the outside world would ever meet him or his people was if he went to them. He held his empty hands open on his lap and wondered when he'd get his chance.

Surviving Village Life

COSMO KICKED THE WITHERED carcass with his foot. Nothing remained of the blackbird except feathers, sinew and a beak. "We've got to find something to eat. I can't make it until dinner."

Ramrei joined his brother at the edge of the dirt road and stared at the desiccated bird.

School had dismissed minutes earlier. After Cosmo and Samuel had changed from their navy blue and white uniforms into their everyday clothing, Ramrei had met them outside the school house. His responsibility was to escort the boys into Low Town, the village colony where their clan resided. Instead, the three boys had taken a circuitous route to nowhere in particular.

"Didn't you have lunch?" Samuel asked the question without turning aside to join the brothers.

Ramrei and Cosmo shifted their gaze from the bird to their sometime friend, Samuel. Cosmo seared him with angry eyes.

"What?" The look on Samuel's face revealed he already knew his offense. Of course he did. The vast majority of the villagers only ate two meals a day. Cosmo never attended school with a lunch. Today there had hardly been any breakfast—a few chickpeas and peppers.

Ramrei broke the silence. "Nothing in the jungle is in season, and the village is picked over."

"We could steal something," Samuel offered.

The brothers looked at him then shrugged. It wouldn't be the first time they'd nicked something from a backyard. Stolen or not, it filled the stomach the same.

Cosmo looked to his brother and raised a brow.

Ramrei nodded. "High Town."

Samuel barked and clutched for the brothers' arms. "I meant around here, in Middle Town. I don't want to get beat up."

Cosmo shook off Samuel's grip. "A good idea is a good idea."

Ramrei led the way toward the hillside on the east of town. The valley they lived in sloped upward gradually as it followed the course of the river. None of the village was so steep that the rains eroded it, but just enough that the clans in High Town were able to look down on the rest. "I'm not going to steal from Middle Town when I can just as easily take from those sods in High Town."

Samuel stomped his flip-flop in the middle of the road. "Haven't we pissed them off enough lately?"

"We could always leave you here." Cosmo fell in behind his brother's quick march eastward and upward.

Samuel carefully scanned the neighborhood surrounding him. All the adults were either working in the fields or selling vegetables and baskets in the nearest town. The whole village would operate under gang law for at least two more hours.

Samuel had few to no rights under such a system, and he knew it. He jogged to catch up. "On second thought, we don't have to steal. I think there's some food lying around my house."

Cosmo sneered at the pudgy boy. Nearly one year Cosmo's elder, Samuel remained dominated by fear. Sadly, the boy was one of Cosmo's better friends, despite his softness and constant sniveling.

Cosmo ignored most of Samuel's whining, but this latest comment incensed him. What kind of person left food lying around? "We can't all rely on the central government for handouts."

"And what is that supposed to mean?" Samuel gasped.

Ramrei called over his shoulder. "It means you eat from the hand of India, nitwit."

"My father is a teacher! He earns everything he brings home."

"Does he?" Cosmo would have laughed if he wasn't so angry. "If your father is a teacher, who does he teach?" He stabbed a finger toward the government school building, visible beyond a row of stepped huts.

Dried and chipping mud revealed the bamboo beneath. Sections of thatch had blown off during the last rainy season. Abandoned for over a year, the only function the government school building served was to mask the inappropriate behavior of village teens.

Occasionally a handful of children seemed to gather for instruction. Cosmo couldn't figure why. Mainly the building functioned as a constant reminder of how the government of India meddled in every aspect of their life.

Samuel protested. "It's not my father's fault there aren't any students at the government school."

On a roll, Cosmo continued his rebuff. "Have you ever considered the reason there aren't any students might have something to do with the fact there isn't a teacher?"

"*You* don't even go there," Ramrei added.

Samuel huffed and crossed his arms over his chest. "Have you ever considered the reason you don't have any friends is that you are so offensive?"

"I have friends," Cosmo said.

"If you're counting me, you should refigure your numbers."

"Shut up, you two." Ramrei raised his hand. "I think I found something."

Cosmo's stomach lurched at the thought of food. "What is it?"

Ramrei pointed with his chin. "What does that look like to you?"

Cosmo smelled the meat before eyeing it. "Smoked dog." Hung from a porch beam, the dog dangled less than a meter over the dying embers of what used to be a large fire.

Samuel closed his eyes and breathed deeply. "It does smell good."

"Then we're agreed, Cosmo and I will stand watch while you slice off three pieces." Ramrei jabbed Samuel with an elbow and pointed at a knife stuck in a butcher block.

"What? I'm not the one who—"

Cosmo pushed him. "Stealing was your idea."

"I only suggested we—"

"Forget it. I can't wait." Cosmo hurried across the road and leapt the drainage ditch. Before he reached the butcher block, angry words stopped him short.

"What are you Low Towner's doing snatching food from my auntie?"

Cosmo's heart sank into his empty gut as he turned toward the gang of toughs from the Woleng Clan. Cosmo and his brother had run amok of this particular gang before—with poor results.

Subtly, Cosmo narrowed the gap between himself and his brother. While not as talented as Aring, Ramrei was a competent fighter, better than any High Towner. Aring had been teaching both of them the basics despite their father's strict orders not to fight. Samuel was worthless. That put the numbers at one and a half versus a dozen. In other words, not good.

"You guys never learn." The lead boy, a brute by the name of Achan, slapped a bamboo cane against the palm of his hand, then used the stick to scratch his chin. "It looks like we're going to have to beat you this time."

Samuel whimpered and burst into a sprint toward home.

"Round him up!" Achan ordered a few members of his crew to pursue the coward.

Ramrei stared at Achan as the gang shrank to eight. "Just as I planned. Now the numbers are in our favor."

Achan scoffed while exchanging a smirk with his minions.

Instantly, Ramrei launched a front kick into Achan's chest that knocked him off his feet.

Slow to act, Cosmo threw an unfocused punch that resulted in being shoved into his brother.

"Run!" Ramrei clutched the back of Cosmo's shirt and propelled him toward Middle Town.

The smack of a bamboo stick resounded off Ramrei's back as he sheltered his younger brother from the blow.

"Get 'em!" From the ground, Achan ordered the attack.

Without looking back, the brothers ran. The rumble of bare feet in pursuit slapped the dirt. Seconds later, their retreat ended abruptly as they barreled into the detachment who'd already detained Samuel.

Lowering his head, Cosmo bulled one of the boys over before tangling his feet and sprawling face first. In a cloud of dust, the beating commenced in earnest. Feet, fists and sticks pounded the back, butt and sides of the three boys as they tucked into balls the best they could.

Seconds stretched into what felt like minutes. Cosmo's rage overrode his fear. The pain evolved to numbness as his mind fled his body.

"Enough!" Achan coughed, still trying to regain his breath after Ramrei's kick.

The single word jolted Cosmo's awareness, and electricity filled every inch of his body.

"They've learned their lesson. Let them up."

The clump of boys parted.

Careful to disguise the pain on his face, Ramrei rose and helped the two younger boys to their feet. Without a word, the three of them staggered out of High Town.

Minutes later, the boys passed the dead bird on their way home. His adrenaline flagging, Cosmo grew hungrier than ever. Along with his stomach pangs, a dozen new wounds screamed for his attention. And yet, despite the unfortunate afternoon, Cosmo knew the worst was yet to come. He tried not to think about the look on their father's face when he saw his boys' wounds.

Cosmo and his brother stopped for a brief rest as they watched Samuel scamper toward his home, whimpering all the way. Cosmo watched his sometime friend hesitate outside the door of his house.

The structure was in good repair. It was one of the few whitewashed homes in the neighborhood, built mostly from milled lumber. Samuel's family had money to put food on the table and to spare.

Still, Cosmo wouldn't envy a boy he knew would never amount to anything more than a low-level bureaucrat feeding off the oppression of his own people. As the brothers resumed their slow pace homeward, Cosmo gave voice to his creeping fear. "Papa's going to kill us."

Wincing, Ramrei took Cosmo's hand. "We never threw a punch. We were minding our own business. Samuel wanted to show us new classroom supplies at the government school."

"He'll never believe it." Cosmo shook his head.

"Maybe not, but he believes weakness is the answer." Ramrei sighed.

"What about Mahatma Gandhi?"

"You want to know the real lesson from today?" Ramrei asked.

Cosmo briefly pondered his four years of schooling and their father's countless Bible lessons. None of it offered him an obvious lesson from the day's beating. This was exactly the type of lesson he looked to his older brothers for. "Yes."

Ramrei looked straight ahead, the boys' home visible at the end of the dirt road. "Choose your friends from among the strongest of your enemies, not the weakest."

For years, those words echoed in Cosmo's brain louder than any others.

PART 2

MANHOOD IN MANIPUR

Respect and Intimidation

IT SEEMED TO COSMO that every day a new billboard went up around the perimeter of Kangla Park. For the span of three blocks he barely saw past the barrage of advertisements for exotic products he couldn't afford. Some of the advertised goods held no other purpose than status.

Like banners stretched between two-story chopsticks, the flimsy billboards creaked. Peeling edges fluttered in gusts of wind and exhaust. With pleasure, Cosmo followed his gang of comrades away from the park's edge.

At an intersection jammed with bicycles, rickshaws, mopeds and porters pulling makeshift trailers, his thoughts wandered to the jungle. Cosmo knew he should schedule a return trip to his village, if only for his mother's sake.

Somehow, they had managed to send him to boarding school in Imphal City for the last five years. The least he could do was visit them once a year. And yet, he'd already scheduled his upcoming vacation with training and fights. The next vacation seemed too far away to concern himself over, especially given his current lifestyle.

Traffic lurched forward, carrying him with it like driftwood caught in a river current. Standing on the pedals, he pumped hard enough to free himself from the main flow of traffic. Together with the rest of the gang, Cosmo rode to the top of a small rise in a neighborhood on the very edge of the restricted area.

"There they are." The gang's leader, Damu, slammed on the

brakes of his bicycle and skidded to a sideways stop in the middle of the dirt road. From atop the rise, he pointed past a low row of mud homes. "Beneath the bridge."

Cosmo, along with a dozen other members of Damu's gang, stopped beside their charismatic leader. Cosmo nodded. "I knew the Meitei Brothers were expanding their territory."

"It looks like little Cosmo was right." Damu slapped his youngest protégé on the back before turning toward the larger group. "Today, we teach the Brothers a lesson. Tomorrow," he grinned, "we'll teach them again."

The others whooped as Damu waived his arm and led the downhill charge. The ruckus drew the attention of the Brothers, along with a few dozen bystanders on their way to the nearby shopping mall. Heads down, the pedestrians accelerated their pace until no one remained in the way of the rival gangs.

Cosmo dismounted his bicycle before it had come to a complete stop. Constantly wound up, his muscles sprang eagerly into form. Beneath the bridge and next to a fetid drainage canal, the day's street fight bloomed—the gang's first since the day before. As sure as the sun would rise, tomorrow would bring another.

Half an hour later, Damu's gang pedaled their bikes around the southern end of the park, smug with victory and oblivious to the minor wounds they'd incurred during the fight. As they passed a restaurant, one of the older boys, no longer a teen, called from the back. "How 'bout some lunch?"

Without a word, the whole gang agreed. Stacking their bikes against each other, they puffed their chests and ambled inside. The dirty, storefront window lent the dimly lit restaurant an orange hue. The odors of exhaust and garbage instantly gave way to roasted fish and what Cosmo thought to be a hint of cardamom. He filled his lungs. "I'm suddenly in the mood for fresh fish."

As the others rearranged the furniture, Cosmo snatched a handful of fennel seeds from a bowl on the counter. He ground them between his thumb and finger and popped them in his mouth. In the process, he realized blood had dried on his hands.

He spit into them and wiped them on his pants. Afterward, his hands smelled tangy sweet, as if cleansed in expensive perfume. Cosmo pulled up a chair at the far end of the table.

Damu shook his head and gestured for the youngest member of his gang to take the seat next to him.

Proudly, Cosmo obliged while ignoring the grumbles of the older gang members. Cosmo often wondered if the sixteen-year-old Damu kept him around so he wouldn't be the youngest member of his own gang.

Damu picked up the conversation from earlier. "Fish, huh? You know, I've never seen you eat anything other than meat."

"I'll eat vegetables when all the animals are gone."

"Personally, I love a good samosa or spicy shinzhu." Damu stroked his chin. "Or just a fresh tomato sliced thin and sprinkled with salt and coriander. Didn't your mother cook vegetables?"

Cosmo lowered his voice. "Nothing but."

"Ah," Damu nodded, "you're feeding a hunger, not an appetite."

Cosmo remained quiet.

"We're all hungry for something."

Slowly, Cosmo raised a questioning eye. "And you?"

Damu waived for the server then pulled Cosmo close until their heads knocked. "Anyone else asks, I'm hungry for money and power." He breathed deeply. "The truth: I'm hungry for respect. But the virtue seems extinct from among the Manipuri." Damu released his grip on the back of Cosmo's head and resumed his smug smile.

While pondering Damu's words, Cosmo watched the anxious owner of the restaurant intercept the server to wait on their table personally.

Trembling with terror, the man's gaze swept the table. Finally he arrived at Damu as the head. "Your order, gentlemen?"

At Damu's request, Cosmo ordered first. A quick inquiry revealed the odor wafting from the kitchen to be roasted kawoi fresh from Loktak Lake. Cosmo nodded. With a glance at Damu, he ordered a kachumber salad on the side.

The owner of the restaurant struggled against his quaking hand to scrawl the order into his notebook. Cosmo puzzled at the man's behavior. Not one member of the gang had harassed the man, and yet he seemed on the verge of bolting out the back door.

Damu ordered last—dum aloo.

Bowing and smiling profusely, the trembling owner retreated into the kitchen.

Damu elbowed Cosmo and chuckled beneath his breath.

Cosmo followed along, but still couldn't figure the strange behavior. Giving up the puzzle, he joined in the banter as his comrades relived the most glorious moments of the day's fight.

Laughing and drinking bottled water, they poked fun at each other's scrapes and bruises. Only then, did Cosmo make the connection. The server shuttled each of them a glass of ice. Cosmo put two cubes in his hand and held them to his cheek.

As bloody rivulets of anise-scented water coursed down his neck, he glanced at each member of the gang. Cuts, scrapes, and bruises had become a regular part of life to them. Bloodstains and torn clothing were a badge of honor.

To onlookers, the blood simply meant trouble. Without trying to intimidate, they scared people who ran away from fights rather than toward them. Grinning and puffed up with his new knowledge, Cosmo offered the rest of his glass of ice to Damu.

After the food had come and gone, the owner surprised Cosmo again by refusing to charge them for anything they'd eaten. This was an interesting revelation indeed.

Training a Warrior

THE SUN CRESTED THE horizon, its light falling lightly across Cosmo's cheek. He opened his eyes with a start. The open-air jungle dormitory was empty. He had slept in again. Dreading the cane on the palms of his hands or souls of his feet, he leapt out of bed and bolted toward the wild banana grove where the master often taught.

Across an open field, he saw the rest of the students kicking the trunks of banana trees. As he neared, he realized his master was sitting cross-legged high up in a tree—supported by nothing more than a banana leaf and thin air. Cosmo slowed his approach.

Temporarily forgetting the potential punishment for sleeping in, he stared up at his master. "How are you doing that?"

The master responded without shifting his gaze. "Obey every word of my teaching, and I will open up to you all the powers of the black arts."

A shiver ran down Cosmo's spine. Risking further punishment, he spoke again. "If you please, I prefer only to learn techniques for combat."

"Very well. Beneath the big banana tree, in deep horse stance, begin with 1,000 repetitions of Yin and Yang circular waves."

Obediently, Cosmo trotted off and began the work. The clean air strengthened him with every breath. Eyes closed, he progressed through the repetitions.

Always synchronized with the earth, he never rushed his movements. He allowed his body to flow at its own pace. The stronger he became, the quicker that pace. The quicker the pace, the more power he delivered without sacrificing balance.

Immune to the heat and separate from fatigue, he repeated the Yin and Yang motions for half an hour. Only the count remained in his thoughts—the single reminder his mind and body remained connected. *One Thousand.*

He lowered his arms and held them at his waist, elbows bent, fingers loose. He straightened his knees and opened his eyes.

"Now a lesson in combat, as you wish." His master handed him a bamboo stick. "Attack me at full speed."

Cosmo whipped the stick at his master's head.

Before Cosmo could register the movements, his master had dodged to the side, stepped forward and knocked Cosmo to the ground. "Again."

Cosmo rose to his feet. Gripping the stick, he repeated the same motion more quickly.

Not even bothering to dodge, the master extended both hands into Cosmo's solar plexus. The power of the blow lifted Cosmo off the ground and stole his breath. He hadn't come close to landing a blow.

"Now that you know how not to strike, practice how to strike correctly."

For the next hour, Cosmo practiced by himself. At noon, the master requested Cosmo kick down the banana trunk and carry it to the dorm for the midday meal. Cut up and mixed with Naga spices and steamed rice, the trunk provided food enough for everyone.

Days later, Cosmo accompanied his master into the city for medicine and cooking oil. From across the street, a rival gang recognized Cosmo. Of course the gang failed to recognize the strength of the old man, and the depth of the training he had imparted to his student.

The gang leader closed in on Cosmo. Swinging a chain with lethal force, his initial attack nicked Cosmo's ear.

Outnumbered and unarmed, Cosmo eliminated the gang leader with a double strike to his groin and throat.

As the second attacker bore down on Cosmo with an arm-length section of pipe, his master cried out, "Take the bar!"

Without a second thought, Cosmo struck the attacker in the eyes and seized the pipe. Gripping it in both hands, Cosmo spun into the attacker, elbowed him in the face and wrenched the pipe out of his hands.

He checked on his master, only to discover he had snatched a bar himself. Together, the two of them used the sections of pipe like swords—applying a basic Thaing offense. After they dropped a half-dozen attackers, the remainder turned and fled.

Cosmo scanned the gang members lying on the ground to ensure none of them were a threat. In the distance he spotted several police. Ignoring the cries and groans of the fallen thugs, Cosmo and his teacher ducked behind the nearest store and disappeared into the jungle.

They would have to return the next day for medicine and oil.

Note to Reader: Blank Pages Ahead

THERE ARE SECTIONS TO skim and even skip in everyone's life story. Most often these sections are bypassed due to their status as mundane, redundant and/or irrelevant in context to the larger story. The same is true of Cosmo Zimik's story.

But, unlike the rest of us, Cosmo's story also contains sections that must be passed over for his safety and the safety of those he loves. It is also vital this book do no harm in his continued efforts to improve the physical and spiritual conditions of his people.

In some instances, masking sensitive information is as simple as changing or concealing the names of people, places and dates. Astute readers might note throughout the text a lack of specifics when it comes to military forces, "militants" or investigative governmental agencies.

This lack of detail, while unfortunate, is necessary to avoid agitating said authorities.

Due to sensitive and continuing circumstances (and Cosmo's desire to continue his work in and around his homeland), I have skipped over or euphemized aspects of Cosmo's life. I apologize in advance for declawing aspects of the story. Until circumstances change, there is no other choice.

I have chosen this point in Cosmo's story to raise this issue because Cosmo's late teens proved too difficult to easily obfuscate. Instead, I've chosen the more disappointing (yet practical) option of skipping them entirely.

And so, dear reader, as you've been reading this aside, nearly three years have passed in Cosmo's life. The sixteen-year-old Cosmo you last knew is now nineteen. It must suffice for me to say those three years were dark and violent ones during which Cosmo both dealt and suffered abuse. Each act of violence inched him further along a path he would have recoiled from had it revealed itself all at once. But as they say, if you want to cook a frog, don't throw it into a boiling pot.

On that note, I'll return you to Cosmo's story moments before one of its lowest points—the same point I chose for the opening of the book.

At the End of an AK-47, Take Two

BY THE TIME COSMO reached the community center, dancing Jeep headlights were visible through the jungle canopy on the edge of the village. Without slowing down, Cosmo kicked in the paneled door of the community center, knocking it from its bottom hinges.

He skidded to a stop and scoured the dark for his things. They weren't where he'd left them. Something didn't feel right. He stretched his ears for any indication of human presence. What he heard was the release of the charging handle of an AK-47 as it chambered a 39mm cartridge.

Cosmo sprang toward the open doorway as the single-room community center sparked to life with the flame and roar of gunfire. After striking the door jam with his shoulder, Cosmo tumbled into the street and landed on all fours.

Quickly scrambling to his feet, he struck a path for the nearest shelter. Behind him, the single AK-47 spawned into several as gunfire erupted from the moving Jeeps. Through ringing ears, Cosmo heard angry shouts. They were closing in, but the bullets remained erratic.

With a final leap, he ducked behind a hut and didn't slow down. He burst through a low picket fence consisting of half-rotten boards and darted across another dirt road under the creeping light of dawn.

A Jeep's headlights swept across him, followed immediately by gunfire. He altered his course. Abandoning his effort to reach the nearest hut, he chose instead to head for the nearest trees. The flimsy bamboo and mud huts wouldn't provide much cover, and Cosmo didn't want to get bystanders killed, if he could help it.

A second Jeep flanked him.

He dug inside for a reserve of strength, but he'd tapped the very depths the moment he heard the clack of the charging handle in the community center. Just another thirty meters and he'd reach the tree line. *Almost there.*

Before he'd gone three strides, another source of gunfire exploded from the shadow of a nearby hut—twice as close as the Jeeps. The first rounds struck the ground in front of Cosmo. Instinctively, he dove.

This wasn't how it was supposed to go. He wasn't supposed to die in the dark in some nameless village. This wasn't a fair fight. This was murder.

Dirt pelted Cosmo's face as bullets bit into the ground all around him. Driven by instinct, he dug his feet into the rutted surface and lurched upward like a sprinter from the blocks. Leaning too far forward, his muscles screamed to lift and drop each foot fast enough to keep him upright—to keep running.

The air turned to soup. Cosmo clawed at it with his hands. Thick as sludge, the darkness tugged at him, dragging him down. He refused to succumb. Each second stretched impossibly long.

Less than a dozen meters from the protection of the jungle, a hornet's sting tore into the meat of Cosmo's thigh. The leg faltered. He pitched sideways and crashed to the ground short of safety.

In shock, operating on survival instinct alone, Cosmo clawed his way forward with his three remaining limbs. Headlights illuminated him along with the trees just out of reach. The gunfire stopped.

Voices and footfalls approached from behind. In a final desperate effort, Cosmo raised his eyes and searched the jungle for friendly faces. Grasping at straws, he thought perhaps Damu had heard the Jeeps and returned to save him. Nothing but empty shadows greeting him.

An AK-47 fired from extremely close range. "Stay down!"

Out of options, Cosmo dropped to his stomach and protected the back of his head with his hands. A moment later, the butt of a rifle cracked into his skull, breaking his fingers in the process.

Healing Never Comes Easy

THE TORTURE LASTED LONG enough to lose meaning. After the first day, Cosmo couldn't remember why it was happening or what his captors wanted. Half the time, no one seemed to know. By the third day, he couldn't remember anything.

Finally, he slinked inside a cave in the back of his mind and went to sleep. The violence and pain continued. He felt every bit, but kept no record. Each blow, shock or cut erased the one preceding it. And so he killed his past a moment at a time.

Then, with effort, he erased the future.

But the pain remained, anchoring him to the present.

Until without announcement, it stopped.

When the pain returned, it came carrying snatches of memory. Fragments. Cosmo saw the faces of his captors. He saw Damu disappear into the dark—*may the jungle conceal your presence*. His friend's parting words, the last friendly words he'd heard, echoed in Cosmo's brain.

He tried to push his awareness beneath the surface—to remain asleep in his mental cave. But too much sensory data filtered through the veil. The pain had dulled, leaving room for exploration and discovery. He smelled the freshness of the jungle. He heard gentle, rhythmic humming—a tune.

With that realization, his conscious mind rebooted. His awareness returned to his broken body. Against his will, he felt the full intensity of the physical pain, along with the emotional pain of abandonment.

He struggled with his eyes, the left one swollen shut and the right one crusted over. After a steady flow of tears, it broke open. Without moving his head, he methodically studied his surroundings for what could have been hours.

He decided it safe to turn his neck. Pain and stiffness allowed for only the slightest of movement. He rested.

The humming returned. Cosmo opened his functioning eye. This time an elderly woman greeted him with a smile. "Do not try to move. You've been hurt very badly. Including your spine. It will take time for the swelling to go down."

Cosmo attempted to move his toes, but could not. *I'm paralyzed.* His breathing and pulse increased.

The woman cocked her head and stared into his eye.

"Who are you?" Cosmo asked.

"I'm not with whoever did this to you. That is all you need to know."

"Don't you want to know who *I* am?"

The woman scoffed. "Why would I?"

"I could be a bad guy."

"And are you?"

"Am I what?" Cosmo became confused.

"A bad guy?"

The question stung Cosmo deeper than he would have imagined. It stung even worse that he knew the answer instantly. It took him several moments to admit it. "Yes. I am a bad guy."

The old woman tutted. "Lucky for me, you are incapacitated, and will be for many days. Maybe by the time you can stand, time will have changed you."

Cosmo knew better. Time alone could not change him. The sermons of his childhood flooded his mind in a jumble. No single word or thought rose above the confusion, just a sense of sorrow.

For the first time, Cosmo prayed to the God of his father. *I'm sorry, God, for ignoring you. But I promise, let me walk again and I will do nothing but good things. Let me walk again, if only to apologize to my parents for all the wrongs I've done.*

Cosmo's functioning eye continued to water. He closed it to rest.

The sounds of the jungle came and went for an indeterminate period. Among the nightmares from his past, Cosmo's sleep often incorporated tender moments he'd spent with his mother and father. The old woman's tune wove it all together. Her humming mutated and took on new complexities. Gradually, it took on colors and images.

One day, as Cosmo focused on the tune, he felt the woman changing the bandages around his leg. Coughing, he strained to lift his head. "I feel that."

The woman nodded and went about her work without interrupting her tune.

Cosmo lay back and swallowed. *I'm getting better. I'll walk again.* On the heels of his first positive thought in days, possibly weeks, guilt and fear redoubled their efforts. "I should have died. You should have let me."

The woman stopped her humming. "Your death is a certainty, young man. But when it happens is not for me to decide. Death will always take its course with or without our help. Life requires us to fight. Perhaps you should reconsider your loyalties." With the flat side of a blade, the woman smeared something hot and damp on his wounded thigh.

Cosmo's eyes swam. The nauseous odor choked his lungs. The weight of her words choked his heart. "I only wanted to stand up to them. I wanted to take back what they've taken from me."

The woman finished with his leg and deposited the leftover poultice on a cluttered table. "Did you get it?"

Cosmo shut his eyes tight. He didn't understand what she was asking. His mind remained sluggish. "Get what?"

"The things they took from you? Did you get them back?" She shuffled to his side and shifted the pillow beneath his head.

Cosmo pinched his eyes tighter in an effort to hold back tears.

The last time he remembered crying was…he couldn't remember a time at all.

"It's time to roll you over." With warm hands, the woman stuffed a rumpled sheet beneath his back. She shifted to the other side of the bamboo bed. Gripping the sheet, she slowly used it to roll Cosmo onto his stomach. Then she stood back and tutted. "There's a difference between standing and taking, child. You can do the one with empty hands and a pure heart. Not the other."

His face buried in the pillow, Cosmo could no longer hold back the tears. The woman's words jolted him more violently than any method of torture. In the span of a second, he relived all the moments of emptiness from his childhood—his empty stomach, his empty pockets, his empty hands helpless to do anything about it.

He heard his younger self speaking the vow to never show weakness and to never forgive those who do. He blamed his father and the passive teachings of Jesus for letting others victimize him and his family. All the backbreaking labor his mother was still forced to endure. If God cared for them, why didn't he protect them?

"You're still alive." The old woman's voice interrupted his internal ramblings. "Maybe you'll learn the difference yet."

Cosmo leaned on his handmade crutch and turned for a final look at the hut where he'd spent the last several weeks. He couldn't be sure how long the old woman had cared for him, any more than he could be sure he'd see the woman again. Vaguely, he hoped for the opportunity to pay her back for saving his life.

The woman had already disappeared inside her hut.

Through the dense jungle, Cosmo couldn't see any other huts or signs of human life. The woman claimed the nearest village to be over a kilometer west. She pointed Cosmo north after providing him with a few landmarks to guide him toward a jungle road that would eventually wind its way back to civilization.

"Thank you." In the absence of the woman, Cosmo spoke the words to the jungle in her stead. Then he began a steady and painful march that would in time loosen his muscles and clear his mind.

History: Oinam and Operation Bluebird

CEASEFIRES AND DECLARATIONS ASIDE, most Nagas consider their war with India perpetual and without pause since 1956 to the present. If acts of violence between the Naga and the Government of India are any indication, the continuous war assessment appears to be correct. Also, one can regard the Armed Forces Special Powers Act of 1958, which is still in effect throughout the Nagalim, as further evidence the war is ongoing.

Indeed, it's obvious the violent conflicts didn't cease after the ceasefire of 1964. The largest example of post 1960's violence occurred in the hills of Oinam in 1987. Many Nagas remember the event as the Oinam War or Oinam Massacre. Indian authorities remember it as Operation Bluebird.

Whatever its name, the current generation of Nagas live with the events from Oinam emblazoned upon their psyche. For any Naga alive at the time, the events at Oinam continue to galvanize their resistance to the Indian government. While these events happened over a year before Cosmo Zimik was captured and tortured, they impacted him deeply and personally.

The record shows that on July 9th, 1987, Naga freedom fighters (they are recognized as such by the United Nations) raided a post of the Assam Rifles (the branch of Indian military most often assigned to border and tribal areas) near the village of Oinam, Manipur. In broad daylight the Naga troops killed 9 Assam Rifle soldiers (known as Jawans) and strode off with large amounts of munitions.

In an effort to recover the looted items, the Assam Rifles launched Operation Bluebird. But as the operation unfolded, it became widely regarded as retaliation and/or revenge more than a systematic search for stolen goods.

Over a span of four months, the Assam Rifles quarantined an area including some thirty villages and subjected their Naga residents to torture, rape, sexual molestation, beatings and summary executions. According to firsthand accounts, two women were forced to give birth to their children publicly in front of the Jawans.

Multiple accounts of these atrocities have been provided by Naga villagers and recorded by human rights organizations. In 1990, Amnesty International wrote an extensive report titled, "Operation Bluebird: A Case Study of Torture and Extrajudicial Executions in Manipur."

Within the report, villagers describe being kept outdoors in the rain and heat for weeks on end. They claim older villagers died from the stress of exposure. More than a hundred houses, churches and school buildings were allegedly burnt or dismantled. Crops failed. Villagers were forced into hard labor building roads and internment camps. During all of this, it is believed not a single stolen weapon was recovered.

Locals and activists appealed to the regional government in Manipur, but the Chief Minister declared the Assam Rifles a rogue entity riding roughshod over the rule of law. Indeed, in some instances the Rifles imprisoned local police and threatened anyone who got in their way.

And so Operation Bluebird continued until the end of October, 1987—nearly four months. Within a year, charges were leveled against the Assam Rifles. This, in and of itself, was a historic occurrence due to the protection bequeathed them by the Armed Forces Special Powers Act. In July of 1988, the High Court of India directed the sessions judge in Imphal, Manipur to record evidence primarily consisting of eye-witness accounts.

Due to a large intimidation campaign carried out by the Assam Rifles, only 22 witnesses were brought forth. Even so, the extensive testimony of those individuals took many weeks to record. From 1988 to 1992, the Assam Rifles filed counter claims, made criminal charges, harassed countless individuals assisting the Naga, identified over 700 witnesses on their behalf, and in general did whatever they could to derail the judicial process.

In 1992, the presiding judge recorded a 10,000 page brief only to be transferred before he could record the final judgment. Twenty-one years later, no judge has been appointed to take his place, and the case is still pending.

I've Been Expecting You

FOR A WEEK, COSMO traveled slowly and in short increments—his progress always in the general direction of home. He'd decided on the destination subconsciously and out of default.

He couldn't stomach the thought of returning to school or running into Damu. In all likelihood, his old gang considered him dead. He might as well leave it that way. Besides, he had already garnered enough education to qualify for university, if he decided to attend.

Cosmo had to admit, as readily as he had left the village behind, the village had refused to leave him. So it was, the prodigal son returned home. With a body slowly healing and a hopelessly shattered spirit, Cosmo beheld his parents' hut for the first time in nearly two years.

Having ditched the crutch midway through his travels, Cosmo centered his weight between both feet and did his best to stand tall. He did not want his mother to embrace a broken child. He breathed deeply and rapped on the door.

He waited, then knocked again. Mud had crumbled from around the door without being repaired. Not only was the bamboo exposed, but Cosmo could have slipped rupees through several of the cracks, had he a single coin to his name.

No one answered. Cosmo heard singing from the back. With as little limp as possible, he followed the source of the song—a favorite hymn of his father's. For the first time, he made a connection between his father's hymn and the old woman's humming. The tune wasn't exactly the same, but similar enough to be a regional variation.

Cosmo stopped several meters short of the garden where his father stooped in labor. Weeds outnumbered the crops. The prodigal tried to clear his throat to greet his father, but he lacked the words.

Suddenly his father straightened. Smiling, yet sad, he looked directly at his youngest son. "Cosmo, I've been expecting you."

The Prodigal Meets King David

AS INDEPENDENT AS COSMO had become since leaving home —as confident and unyielding as an unblemished bamboo cane—his father's words struck him like a typhoon snapping every tree in the jungle. Cosmo teetered on weak knees.

The older man moved more intentionally than Cosmo remembered. The father sat his basket aside, brushed his hands on his pants, and steadily closed the space between father and son.

He continued the hymn at a hum, his hands held out as if attempting to soothe and corral a stray pig. Somehow the father knew the temptation to run coursed through the son's trembling limbs. Before the son could react, the father wrapped his arms around him, as if Cosmo was a child.

The father placed his lips to the son's ear and whispered softer than a mosquito. "I know of all the things you've done, my son. God has shown me the path you've trod."

Cosmo's weak knees folded. Blood pounded in his temples. His vision blurred.

The father gripped the boy to his chest. "The lust for violence, the greed, the pride. It's been a windy road, but God has brought you home."

Dangling in the father's embrace, the son breathed a single word, "How?"

The father draped the son's arm over his broad shoulders. Together the pair hobbled toward the weathered bench propped against the back of the hut. "Did you think for a second God was not with you?"

Cosmo shook his head, a distant vacancy in his eyes. "They tortured me."

For the first time, the father quaked beneath the son's weight. "Especially then. Did you not survive an ordeal that should have killed you a dozen times?"

As father and son dropped onto the creaking bench, a memory blossomed in Cosmo's mind. He remembered praying to God while lying paralyzed on his back in the old woman's hut. He remembered promising his service in exchange for his life.

"Every action has its consequence, son. God cannot save us from our own choices. But he promises to preserve the most important part, if we surrender it to him."

"So I suffered violence because of the violence I've done to others." Cosmo gritted his teeth. "It's just karma in Christian clothing." His eyes roved the familiar tree line at the edge of the village.

"No." His father breathed deeply. "Perhaps I failed to tell you often enough when you were a child—you need to understand, son, I love you."

Cosmo clenched his eyes shut, and the world began to spin.

"No matter what you've done, I love you with all the love God has enabled me. Yet my love is imperfect. I'm petty, selfish, quick to anger and slow to forgive. Not so with God. Nothing you do can erode his love, or earn it."

"Then it's hopeless." Cosmo opened his eyes. He saw neither the jungle sloping gently uphill nor the trees composing it. He didn't feel the light breeze waft beneath the thatch-covered porch where he and his father sat. He didn't feel anything.

His father shook his head. "I've been so frightened of awakening violent spirits from our people's past, I've neglected to teach you the whole of the Gospel story."

Cosmo didn't flinch. "Jesus died on a cross. He let the Jews and the Romans kill him. I know the story."

"No, in the Old Testament there was a king by the name of

David. He was a warrior with blood on his hands."

Cosmo's spine tingled. For the first time in months a sharpness of focus flooded his mind.

His father continued. "David grew up fighting from a young age. Men flocked to his leadership. He trained them into a small army. God had promised David the Kingdom of Israel, and yet Israel already had King Saul—a mighty man, impressive in the eyes of others.

"While small and unimposing physically, David's heart impressed God. For years, David remained God's chosen king while Saul lived in the palace and David lived in caves. Forced to cling to God, David fought against his enemies and his friends. He even joined his enemies to save those under his care."

"Why?" Confusion and anger roiled beneath Cosmo's surface. "Why not just give David the kingdom? Why does God enjoy tormenting his servants?"

"God loved Saul as well." His father turned Cosmo's head until their eyes met. "Don't you understand? God is not just the god of those who serve him. All of this," he gestured toward the village and the hills surrounding them, "the Naga, the Kuki, the Indian, the Burmese, the Hindu, the Muslim, the Animist—God is the creator and lover of them all."

Cosmo stared a long silent moment into his father's eyes. Could he know how Cosmo felt about the poverty God had permitted them to suffer all these years? Of all the horrible things Cosmo had done, how many of them had been for money and for the respect money brings? Now his father was telling him God permitted their poverty because he loved the Indians and Burmese too?

His father blinked first. "I suppose that is a matter for another day. As for Saul, he could not understand how sometimes pleasing God means disappointing the people who rely on us. Saul's trust in the divine failed, so God's anointing failed Saul. He and his son fell in battle, and finally David became king.

"David's years of hardship had equipped him to succeed where Saul had failed. The wilderness had taught him the balance of being a humble warrior. For many years longer than his time in the wilderness, David ruled from the palace. But in time, his spirit grew weak as he grew proud.

"And this is the important part." His father clutched Cosmo gently by the scruff of his neck. "It was said of David that no other man to walk the face of the earth approached closer to the very heart of God. And yet, David strayed.

"While lounging lazily on the roof of his palace, he eyed the bathing wife of another man—one of his loyal generals. He lusted for her. His insides burned like kindling until he devised a strategy to murder the woman's husband and take her as his own.

"Sloth, envy, greed, lust and murder." His father paused for dramatic tension. Even while speaking to his son, he could not disassociate from the practices of his preaching profession. "What would you expect God to do with such a man? A man who had once been closer to him than a son to a father?"

Cosmo could envision the outcome in his head, although he feared the moral of such a story. "The family of the man David murdered would rise up to overthrow his rule. The woman he stole would despise him. There would be a cycle of violence where there had once been peace."

Cosmo's father pursed his lips and nodded, as if processing a new revelation about his youngest son. "If that had been the case, indeed our lives would be hopeless. But that is not what happened." He softened his expression. "God convicted David of his evil doing through the words of a prophet.

"Remembering the closeness he once had with God, David asked forgiveness, which God readily gave. As consequence of David's actions, the ill-conceived child in the woman's womb died. In an act of God's grace, the younger brother of that child grew up to rule in David's place."

Cosmo didn't understand. "David kept his kingdom? But what did he do to earn it back? Did he pay in the afterlife?"

"He did three simple things. He wept, he prayed, he surrendered his life again to God. There is no penance, no karma—not now or in the life to come. There is only our repentance and God's loving grace."

Cosmo held up his hands. Normally steady, they shook. "But what about the blood?"

His father stood and gripped Cosmo's hands in his own. "Washed clean."

Cosmo tightened his grip.

"But you must empty them, son. There is no grasping in God's kingdom, and only empty hands can receive." The father drilled his son with his eyes. "You've wept. You've prayed. But you still have to surrender."

Cosmo's father stood above him. He assumed a gentle air, as if not to send Cosmo fleeing into the jungle on a crippled leg. "Can you do that? Will you?"

Cosmo flirted with releasing his hopelessness, but over the last weeks, the guilt had dug in its claws. How could he not do something to make it right? How could he pretend the blood wasn't there? His father had told him more than he longed to hear. That was exactly the problem. It exceeded the ridiculous.

How could such forgiveness exist in the world Cosmo knew? Surely if he accepted such forgiveness, it would change him. It would change everything. "I," he stuttered, "I want to."

His father nodded. Kneeling in the dirt, he placed his hands over the bullet wound to Cosmo's thigh. "So you know God's presence always comes in power, let this be an outward sign of the work done in your heart on this day."

Cosmo had heard his father speak the same words dozens of times during revival meetings. Never before had they borne meaning. He thought his thigh burned hot beneath his father's hands. Perhaps he imagined it. Then his entire body stiffened.

He closed his eyes and held his breath until he could hold it no longer. Behind closed lids he watched amorphous images and ghastly whiffs of smoke peel away from him and disappear with his exhale. As the breath left his body, so did all the pain, the anger, and the guilt.

He breathed in.

Pulsing with life, he leapt to his feet and pulled his father up with him. He hadn't realized the weight of the burden pressing him toward the center of the earth until it had gone. "Thank you." Cosmo embraced his father for the first time in all his living memory.

His father laughed a belly laugh like that of a man sharing the news of a healthy baby boy after a troubled delivery. "Thank God, for my son had died and now he is alive."

History: Development of the Naga Worldview

WIDE RANGING OPINIONS HAVE been given for the decay of Naga society. Common thought within the Indian government points to drug and alcohol abuse, as well as inter-factional violence, as proof the Naga aren't and have never been capable of self-governance.

It is true, drugs are crossing the border into Nagalim, especially from Burma. It is also true that revenge killings are common among the Naga. The once unified Naga National Council, led by the highly influential Angami Phizo, dissolved in 1953. Two decades later, even Phizo himself became a divisive figure.

When Nagas are asked about these troubling issues, the most common culprit is the Indian divide and rule policy. Due to the recent and fragile nature of Naga nationalism, it is no wonder the government of India should attempt such a strategy.

Nagas had no concept of national identity until the attempted siege by the British. The invasion of their homeland by outsiders forced Nagas to temporarily set aside tribal differences and see each other as brothers. Before the British arrived, Nagas had no specific term for their homeland, or for themselves.

Some of the tribes had gone generations or longer without interaction between each other. The traditional hilltop construction of villages for defensive purposes led to natural isolation. This isolation facilitated the rise of hundreds of dialects, some unintelligible to others. In short, Nagas didn't know each other, outside of local skirmishes and conflicts, until the British thrust them together.

But the Naga people learned quickly. Nagas became the Naga for the first time. Ethnically Mongoloid, they shared very little in common with any of their neighbors, certainly not with their Indian neighbors to the south. Their philosophical, social and spiritual beliefs set them apart even further. No matter the differences existing between Naga tribes, those differences remained minuscule in comparison to their invaders.

Thus, as a hostile invader, it made sense for the Indian government to attack the infantile links between Naga tribes and regions with a series of devastating political moves dating back to 1963.

Before going further, it should be pointed out that depicting the impact of these policies is the easy part. Placing responsibility and blame is much harder. Determining where the onus must be placed on India as a neighboring bully, and where responsibility must be placed on the Naga to overcome any and all aggressive geopolitical policy is a complicated matter of personal opinion—one for another book.

In December 1963, following what has become known as the 16-point agreement, India formed Nagaland, the 16th state of the Indian Union. By encompassing only a fraction of the land occupied by the Naga people, the newly formed state created a new division. In 1972, the international boundary between India and Burma was formalized. Running smack through the middle of several villages, the border divided the Naga again, this time between two nations.

In 1967, some leaders of the Federal Government of Nagaland (the successor of the NNC) broke off with Indian support to form the Revolutionary Military Government. Two years later this entity dissolved and its members become employees of the Indian government.

The Nagaland Legislative Assembly was constituted during this period as yet another rival to the underground Federal Government of Nagaland. Often during the 60's, and with the apparent assistance of the Indian government, lines were drawn and sides were taken between warring Naga factions.

After nearly a decade of war, some of these Naga factions began to court the Indian constitution. For the first time, existence within the

Indian Republic became more appealing. It has been suggested by rivals and critics that these Nagas were blinded by power and affluence from the hand of India. And perhaps some Nagas sought to benefit at their brothers' expense.

In that vein, the Central Indian Government struck its most resounding victory in 1975 with the signing of the Shillong Accord. This agreement has become such a powder keg among Nagas, that uncovering its true historical roots seems impossible only thirty-eight years later. Each of the current Naga factions interprets the event differently.

The content of the accord is clear enough. It called upon the Naga to accept the constitution of India without condition and to lay down arms. It laid forth the same basic demand India had made from the beginning—join the republic.

The only other thing everyone can agree upon is that the accord was signed in Shillong on November 11th, 1975 by the Indian governor of Nagaland and "members of the underground's leadership." Beyond that, everything becomes fuzzy. Many key members of Naga leadership were absent, including Phizo, who had been forced into exile years earlier.

Phizo remained mysteriously silent on the signing of the accord until his death in 1990. Theories abound on why he refused to endorse or refute the accord. For several years Nagas were cast into total confusion. Had they surrendered to the Central Indian Government or not?

In 1980, the National Socialist Council of Nagaland (NSCN) arose in attempt to put the Shillong Accord to rest. Isak Chishi Swu, Thuingaleng Muivah and S.S. Khaplang served as the founding leaders. They derided the Shillong Accord as a betrayal. But by 1988 the newly formed NSCN had split to form the NSCN-IM (Isak and Muivah) and the NSCN-K (Khaplang).

More factions exist today. Many more. While evidence has been uncovered that the Indian government regularly endorses one against the others, Nagas have proven they don't always need India's help to divide themselves.

It was under these divided and contentious conditions that Cosmo Zimik first committed his life to Jesus the Christ. A product of these hostilities, Cosmo left northeast India in 1990, at the age of nineteen, and traveled to Delhi for university. There, he experienced his first wholesale exposure to Indian culture. There, his newfound spiritual beliefs came into direct conflict with his cultural worldview.

PART 3

A NEW CHAPTER IN DELHI

Run-in With a Rickshaw

THE CYCLE RICKSHAW DRIVER mumbled under his breath, as if he didn't possess the ability to stop talking. Or perhaps he feared evil spirits would rush in the moment his stream of filthy swearing ceased to pour out.

Cosmo had come to Delhi two weeks earlier not knowing more than a handful of words in Hindi, but he was learning quickly. Kachui, Cosmo's cousin, had arranged for the two of them to meet a Naga pastor working in New Delhi. During their short trip from campus to the storefront church, Cosmo had heard the driver use one word over a dozen times—*bahadur*.

The obvious meaning of *bahadur* was 'brave,' or 'hero.' The British had used it as an honorary title. A week ago, Kachui had awkwardly explained the word's usage by another rickshaw driver as a blessing. Since then, Cosmo's patience for thinly veneered lies had worn out.

Two days earlier, Cosmo had discovered the truth behind *bahadur's* semantics. Indians used the word as a racial slur for Nepali servants. In this case, it appeared yet another rickshaw driver, otherwise known as a cyclewallah, had failed to distinguish between Nepali and Naga.

With each passing usage of the slur, it became more likely Cosmo would fail to distinguish between Jesus' famous teaching on turning the other cheek and Cosmo's personal code of never letting an insult go unpunished.

A dizzying array of bright advertisements blurred past as the rickshaw sped down a subtle grade. Cosmo attempted to distract himself with his surroundings.

Most of the buildings in this older section of Delhi were two or three stories tall and in varying degrees of construction or decay. It was hard to tell which. It appeared to Cosmo the construction process progressed so slowly that buildings remained in continuous repair. Perhaps they were held together by the billboards plastered over every exterior surface.

Currently, his view of the ads was obstructed by a rat's nest of electrical wiring. His village didn't even have electricity. The Indians didn't seem to know what to do with it. Cosmo wasn't sure about the protocols, but he was sure he could figure out a more efficient system than this.

The rickshaw swerved. Cosmo jerked his attention to the street, where a clump of construction workers attempted to drag a man from the edge of the road. Cosmo caught only a quick glimpse, but it looked as if the man had been dead, or close to it.

Their driver shook his fist and ratcheted up the volume of his continual swearing. Two of the workers straightened long enough to return the verbal abuse. Soon they were drowned out in a city of constant auditory and olfactory attack.

The driver punctuated his diatribe with a rude gesture before turning in his seat enough to smile at Cosmo. His teeth and gums were stained red from chewing betel nuts.

Cosmo stared coldly back until the driver frowned and resumed his undercurrent of breathy swears. Cosmo thought briefly of buying the man another filthy betel nut to get him to shut up.

The driver gripped the handlebars and focused on pedaling the rickshaw.

Cosmo elbowed Kachui, who had been avoiding eye contact for the last few kilometers.

Kachui glanced at Cosmo, a look of apology on his face.

Finally Cosmo deduced what had been bothering his cousin for the last several minutes. It hadn't been the rickshaw's foul language, something standard for every Indian Cosmo had met. More familiar with Delhi's streets, Kachui had quickly observed something Cosmo had missed.

They were on the outer loop of Delhi, heading in almost the opposite direction of their destination. The rickshaw driver had taken the outer ring instead of an inner spoke to charge his unsuspecting *bahadur* passengers twice the rate. Cosmo stewed in the dusty caldron of the rickshaw's back seat until they reached the small church where they'd been bound.

Kachui attempted to address the driver, but Cosmo shoved his cousin out of the rickshaw and exited right behind him. He shielded Kachui while crowding the driver. The man smiled and stood on his pedals with his hand out.

The pits of the driver's shirt were ringed with dark stains. His teeth were crooked and half rotten from betel nuts stuffed with tobacco. His eyes were sleepy and red, his hair greased. And yet, this Indian cyclewallah felt superior enough to insult his paying customers.

Kachui tugged on Cosmo's elbow.

Cosmo broke the silence. "How much?"

The driver smiled even broader. They both knew if a passenger had to ask the fare that the price would go up. "Two hundred rupees."

"How much for the direct route." Cosmo spoke in English.

The driver's smile disappeared, replaced by a stream of cursing eventually punctuated by repeating the same price. "Two hundred rupees. You pay!"

"Cosmo!" Kachui tried to stop the inevitable.

Cosmo's hand twitched. Instead of reaching for his pocket, he jabbed the driver in the face.

Before the man knew what had happened, blood burst from his nose and lip. He staggered and fell from his bike onto the sidewalk.

Cosmo stepped calmly out of the way, so as not to hinder the cyclewallah on his way to the ground.

Kachui threw up his hands in panic. "We can't just, now what do we—"

Cosmo gestured toward the small church front. "Let's meet the man you brought me here to meet." He waved his hands in an effort to focus his cousin's attention, but without success.

Kachui's eyes darted from stranger to stranger as a crowd collected around the bloodied rickshaw driver, who had commenced swearing at the top of his voice and pointing at the two Naga outsiders.

Cosmo placed a hand on Kachui's shoulder. The touch untethered him completely. He bolted in the opposite direction on foot. Rather than chase after his cousin, Cosmo removed eighty-five rupees from his pocket. He held the money up for the bystanders to see.

Stooping next to the frenzied driver, he gripped the man's hand and clamped it around the money.

The driver's eyes darted from Cosmo to the onlookers in confusion.

Cosmo slapped him lightly on the cheek to ensure his full attention. "Friend, you made two mistakes. First, I'm a Naga from Manipur, not Nepal. Second, I have self-respect like all Nagas."

With that, Cosmo stood and parted the crowd. After he wiped the driver's blood off his hand, he determined to find a good cup of tea before finding another rickshaw to carry him back to campus.

Naga Party Life

KACHUI BURST INTO THE common room he and Cosmo shared with two others in one of the university dorms. After slamming the door, he held up two envelopes. "They came."

Rubbing his eyes, Cosmo looked up from his studies. "What came?" It took him a moment to focus across the room. When he did, he leapt over the low table and snatched the envelopes before Kachui could retract them.

"Hey, give me that. One of them is mine!"

Cosmo danced away. Keeping his cousin at bay with one hand, he scanned the letters for the one addressed to him. It was from his brother. "Here." He handed Kachui the other envelope and plopped onto the stained sofa to open his.

Kachui skirted the low table and headed for the kitchen counter. Inside the envelopes, they would each find short letters and money to help with the living expenses of attending university in Delhi. They both knew the amount of money in Cosmo's would be significantly less.

Cosmo's father and older brother both provided what they could. It simply wasn't very much.

Cosmo's roommate, Pemi, poked his head out from a darkened bedroom. He swore while wiping drool from the corner of his mouth. "Keep it down in here. Some of us need to rest up for tonight's party."

"I thought you were resting from last night's party." Cosmo held up the cashier's check for 2,000 rupees, the equivalent of $30 US dollars. It would get him through the final six weeks of exams. If he scrimped and got top dollar from reselling his books, it might be enough for him to return home for a visit.

Pemi staggered into the common room and stretched. "Don't be daft. Last night was simply hanging out with friends. Tonight is the party."

"What's the difference?" Cosmo folded the check and stashed it near the back of his bio-chemistry book. He knew his classmates received up to ten times the amount, but the money only made them wasteful. He was not like his classmates. He would be grateful for the little help he received. He would turn the little into something great.

"The difference? The difference?" Pemi threw up his hands and looked to Kachui. "Can you believe your cousin?"

Kachui shrugged while taking the seat on the couch next to Cosmo. He placed two glasses of water on the low table. "I guess you're going to have to explain it to both of us." Pulling a textbook out of his bag, he opened it.

"How can two people who study so much be so ignorant?" Pemi pretended to bend over and touch his toes. He could only get as far as his ankles.

"There's always more to learn, I suppose." Kachui responded absently.

"Learning. Well, learning. Sure. Learning is one thing. But this," Pemi waved his arms as if orchestrating an invisible symphony, "this studying! This stagnation! Aren't you tired of studying yet?"

Cosmo responded without looking up. "How can I be tired when I'm not finished?"

Pemi stepped over Cosmo and squeezed onto the couch in between the two cousins. "You're finished *when* you get tired."

Cosmo took a drink of water and turned the page in his text. "I'll be finished when I graduate in two more years."

Pemi closed the book. "With that kind of attitude, you might as well be finished now."

Cosmo cracked the vertebra in his neck and shot Pemi a withering look. "What's the event tonight?"

"Come on, roomy. It's the Diwali Festival for God's sake."

"Watch your mouth." Cosmo took another drink. "You're beginning to sound like an Indian."

Pemi rolled his eyes. "Well then what could be better than a Naga Student Union Mixer on a festival night?" He elbowed Cosmo and Kachui both.

Cosmo ran a hand over his face and stood. "You know how I feel about the NSU."

Kachui closed his book and stood as well. "Come on, Cosmo. They're our people."

"Et tu, Brute?" Cosmo quipped.

"I forgot about the mixer." Kachui floundered in an effort to cover his sudden flip-flop on the matter.

"So you agree with Pemi, that we should party instead of study?"

"In this case, yes, I think we should put down the books."

Pemi wrapped an arm around Cosmo's shoulder. "Besides, what's so bad about the NSU?"

"I'm only invited when there's a party or a fight."

"Because those are the only times you'll attend." Kachui pouted.

Cosmo paced into the center of the sparsely decorated common room. "The rest is a waste of time. All they do is talk. They don't have the slightest idea how to actually make a difference."

"And you do?" Kachui threw up his hands.

"Not yet," Cosmo pointed at his books, "but I'm learning."

"There's more to learn at university than books," Pemi said.

Cosmo paced to the window. "I'm learning the rest too, from them." He nodded at the street below their second story dorm room.

Pemi and Kachui shared quizzical looks.

"What else is there to learn from spending all my time surrounded by fellow Nagas? It's the Delhites that prevent our people from their full potential. The Delhites are the only ones who can teach us what we need to know to defeat them."

Kachui opened his mouth to speak, then closed it. He stooped to pick up his glass of water. He took a drink.

Pemi filled the silence. "Okay, you've got a point. What exactly that point is, I'm not sure. But for tonight, forget all that. Your books will still be here in the morning. God knows the Delhites aren't going anywhere. But tonight, we dance. Tonight we meet beautiful girls." He raised an invisible glass in a toast. "Tonight, we party."

Cosmo relented, holding up his glass. "You're paying."

"All will be provided, my friends." Pemi wrapped an arm around each of the cousins. "Tonight is on me."

Introducing the Girl

"THANKS FOR BAILING US out the other night." The president of the Naga Student Union greeted Cosmo, Kachui, Pemi and their other suite mate, Theodore. "And messing those guys up in the process."

"They had it coming." Pemi laughed.

"Maybe so, but you guys are still the ones who gave it to them. As a sign of gratitude, I've got someone I want you to meet." The student president nodded toward a nearby grove of trees, visible by the light of a full moon.

The Naga mixer had been staged in a small park a hundred meters from the cricket field hosting the main Diwali Festivities. Still, the rumbling music made it difficult to pick up every word of a conversation. Currently an Indian band was covering Shot Through the Heart by Bon Jovi.

"He's not a revolutionary, is he?" Cosmo asked.

"*She* is my cousin—a second year from Guwahati."

"Assam?"

The student president shrugged. "I've got an uncle who works there."

Pemi jabbed the student president in the shoulder. "Is *he* a revolutionary?"

"Definitely not." The student president winked at Pemi. "But my cousin has a girlfriend who might be."

"Well," Pemi smiled, "in that case."

Cosmo looked to Kachui.

Kachui nodded. "I think I see Achon over by the drinks. I'll catch up with you two later."

Cosmo leaned close to Pemi's ear. "The revolutionary's yours."

"Perfect." Pemi grinned.

Cosmo bowed slightly to his host. "Lead the way."

"Wonderful. She's been dying to meet you."

"Sonya." The girl bowed, offering her name and hand simultaneously.

Cosmo took it lightly then sat on the ground next to Sonya and her friends. A string of Chinese lanterns led the way through a grove of trees to a more removed section of the park.

"Well, I've got other guests to greet." The student president bowed. "I'm glad I had a chance to thank you in person for the other night." He winked at his cousin. "Don't stay out too late."

After the president left, Pemi cleared his throat.

"Oh, forgive me." Cosmo continued the introductions. "Sonya, this is my roommate and partner in crime, Pemi."

"Honor to meet you, Sonya." Pemi bowed toward Sonya while glancing sideways at the gorgeous, pouty-lipped girl seated next to her.

Sonya picked up the not so subtle hint. "Pemi, Cosmo, this is my girlfriend, Nina. Not much to look at I'm afraid, but—"

Nina elbowed Sonya viciously.

Sonya rubbed her arm while continuing to smile. "Please, join us."

"Again, I'd be honored." Pemi beamed. "But first, should I get us some drinks?"

Cosmo rolled his eyes.

The girls nodded.

"Don't go anywhere. I'll be right back." Pemi chose a ridiculous impersonation of a British nobleman for his exit. The dance of light and shadow cast on his white dress pants from the lanterns lining the path animated the swagger even further.

The girls snickered.

Cosmo never doubted Pemi when it came to girls or drink or cards. In all three cases, Pemi always knew what he was doing.

"So, Cosmo, my cousin tells me you're into martial arts." Sonya leaned into him.

Cosmo smiled and looked up at the moon through the opening in the trees. Perhaps his friends had been right. Taking a small break from his studies would invigorate him for better efficiency the coming day. "You could say that."

The Lure of the Fight

THE SECOND YEAR OF Cosmo's studies began much the same way his first year ended, broken up by a short trip home. The monsoon season had been particularly hot and muggy. Well into August, the humidity and daily temperatures remained high.

During Cosmo's afternoon workout, the temperature on the cricket field hovered around 31 degrees Celsius (88 Fahrenheit). Due to the humidity, the nearby drain from the Yamuna River provided no relief. Immediately after his personal workout, Cosmo transitioned into the martial arts class he taught.

Drenched in sweat, Cosmo led the class through their Thaing disciplines without a word. The central core of his class, a mere five or six students, was hard working and consistent. They showed up on time and pushed themselves to improve. Beyond the core students, a rotating fringe of another dozen drifted in and out of the workouts, depending on how hard they had partied the night before.

Cosmo pushed the thoughts aside and focused his mind on the distant sounds of Delhi. If he allowed them to pour over and through each other, they served as a poor replacement for the peace of the jungle. He kept track of the repetitions on a mental clock at the back of his consciousness without the need for actual numbers or counting. When the moment came, he would stop.

Rising from the mental current, he bowed toward the class. They bowed lower. He sat with his legs beneath him and explained the exercises for the day. Popping up, he called one of the stronger male students forward to demonstrate the techniques they would work on.

After a short demonstration, he broke the dozen students into pairs and worked his way around as they practiced. He liked the sharpening effect of teaching. Breaking down the techniques into fundamentals and then employing the patience and insight to help each student improve never failed to better his own fighting.

Each student incorporated his instruction differently. Personalities not only learned differently, but manifested the same moves differently. Those attentive to detail needed help to free their minds into action. Those drawn to impulsivity required additional lessons in the value of accurate form.

He stopped a gifted female student who tended to be one of the latter. He instructed her to start the process of attacking him the way she had been attacking her partner. Without hesitation she lunged for his throat.

Cosmo blocked her hands. With a quick shuffle forward, he kicked her exposed side and swept her legs. He caught her head while pinning her to the ground at the throat.

Angry at herself and the teacher, she ground her teeth.

Cosmo gave her a second to rein in her temper before helping her to her feet. He nodded, and she resumed her stance. This time, with a personalized mixture of strength and humility, Cosmo corrected her bad form. "Keep your weight on your back leg. Keep your elbow strong and you will dictate your opponent's response. Control yourself first. Control your opponent second."

"Thank you, sir." She bowed, and the two partners returned to their sparring.

As Cosmo moved toward the next pair, he noted a man striding toward them from across the field. Using the public space for class required constant vigilance. Typically, locals referred to the area as the cricket field. In reality the open space served whichever team or club had the muscle to commandeer it. Cosmo's class was still small and inexperienced, so a larger, stronger group could force them to leave.

Certainly this lone man posed no threat. Still, Cosmo watched the man approach through the corner of his eye. He wore a gi, but

Cosmo didn't recognize him from any of the martial arts clubs.

Cosmo corrected two more students before realizing the man had taken a seat on the grass twenty meters away. Thinking the man had come for instruction, Cosmo joined him.

As soon as Cosmo sat, the man spoke. "I've seen you fight at the city martial arts club."

Cosmo nodded.

"Good, to the point then. How would you like to make money with your talents?"

"I've made a little." Cosmo thought he knew where the conversation was headed. If correct, caution would be essential. "Are the regional tournament monies increasing? As it is, the prize money hardly seems worth the time, with classes and all."

The man smiled. "I understand your hesitancy. It's a sign of intelligence." The man thumbed his nose. "The money I'm talking about is significantly better."

"How much better?" Cosmo asked the question fully aware that in two weeks time he wouldn't be able to afford rice.

"A thousand rupees."

Cosmo swallowed. The equivalent of $20 USD would feed him for two weeks.

"For a loss."

"Excuse me?"

The man looked Cosmo in the eyes. "A thousand rupees is the standard pay out, win or lose. Every time you win, the amount increases. Win, half a dozen times," the man rocked his head from side to side, "and win with style, the purse tops out at 10,000 rupees."

Cosmo licked his lips.

"Could you use 10,000 rupees, Mr. Zimik? Because from what I've seen, I wouldn't expect you to lose."

"But I'm a student first. I have class—"

"Most of the fights are on Saturdays, no more than an hour bus ride outside of the city."

Cosmo paused for a deep breath. He watched his class train without him. He had considered fight clubs and prizefights before.

Until now he hadn't known how to find one, much less had an invitation. And the level of prize money shocked him.

The stranger was right about one thing, Cosmo wouldn't lose. That meant $200 USD on a single Saturday, for a few minutes worth of fighting. Two hundred dollars. He could afford real shoes for the first time in his life. He stared at the calloused black soles of his feet and recalled the days in Manipur when the skin had flaked off in white chunks from being wet and mildewed.

"And the rules?" Cosmo asked.

"Well, other than biting or attacking the groin, there are no rules." The man stood suddenly. "Look, most of the locals come from a background in Kushti or some variant. They're farmers and street thugs. The sport needs some discipline. Some exotic talent. I'm paid to find that talent."

Cosmo stood. This wasn't the same as what he'd been a part of before. He wasn't fighting over turf. He'd be beating up Indians in a ring and getting paid for it. Besides, it was either this or find a job as a porter or autowallah. By fighting he could earn ten times the amount of money and still have plenty of time to study. "Where do I go?"

"Good." The man produced a piece of paper and held it out. "Here is the address."

Cosmo took it.

"This Saturday the fights will be in an old barn. Show up by 1:00pm. You'll be paid by 5:00pm." The man looked Cosmo up and down. "How much do you weigh?"

"Seventy-five kilograms."

"We'll start you off as a middleweight."

"Fine. Good." Jittery with excitement, Cosmo bowed.

The stranger returned the bow. "Sorry to interrupt your class."

"No need. Thank you for the opportunity."

"No need." The man spoke over his shoulder while walking off. "Show up, fight, make it look good. We all come out winners."

Cosmo watched the man stride away before returning to his class with a huge grin on his face. Fighting, making it look good, and winning were the three things that came most natural to him.

Delhi Fight Club

COSMO STEPPED OFF THE bus alone. He knew better than to bring his cousin, Kachui, to an event like this. And Pemi would have wanted to get in the ring, or worse, start a fight with someone in the audience. Cosmo waited for the bus to slog out of sight along the muddy road before striding toward a barn visible beyond a farmhouse and a row of palm trees.

Whatever happened in these fights, he wanted to disguise his participation from his family and classmates. Today he was supposed to be on a spiritual retreat in the Central Ridge Forest near downtown New Delhi. The bus he'd taken had passed right by it.

If he received any visible cuts or bruises during the fight, well, he'd have to improvise his story. But the idea that Cosmo Zimik could get into a fight on a spiritual retreat wouldn't seem completely out of the ordinary.

Cosmo stopped short of the barn to consider whether this truth constituted an irreconcilable irony. Should he be upset with himself? Was there something wrong with being an angry Christian who spent so much time fighting? He knew what his father would say.

"Mr. Zimik."

Cosmo recognized the voice from the cricket field.

The man who had invited him poked his head out from behind a large wooden door on tracks. "Don't stand around in the mud looking stupid. There's someone you need to meet."

"Right." Cosmo hurried inside the shadowy barn. The expected odors of manure and hay had been masked by cigarette smoke and disinfectant.

With no further greeting, the man led Cosmo behind some makeshift stands. Seconds later, they entered a side room that looked like it had once stored grain. The cement floor had cracked and worn over the course of several decades, aging the barn as pre-independence, perhaps even World War I.

A white man sat behind a desk in the middle of the room, his head buried in a ledger book. The only light came from a lamp on his desk. The lamp's cracked and stained shade rested crookedly. The lack of ventilation lent the room an oppressive air.

The man who'd invited Cosmo stood at attention beside the desk. No one spoke.

Cosmo waited patiently to be introduced, or inspected, or whatever the protocol in such circumstances called for. He hadn't come here by accident, so as far as he was concerned all of this must be normal for a fighter's first event.

More than a minute later, the man behind the desk showed signs of life by rubbing the back of his neck. After another pause, he raised his head. Removing his glasses, he placed them on the desk and stared at his man. "Get on with it. Is this the college student from the infernal tribal area?" The boss spoke with an English accent.

The man who had invited Cosmo cleared his throat. "Yes. This is Cosmo Zimik, from Manipur."

"Well la di da, a first name *and* a last. Aren't we formal, Mr. Bashir Khan. And the kid's presence in my barn somehow justifies this interruption?"

Khan didn't blink. "I wanted you to meet the best fighter of today's event before your colleagues arrived."

"Well crap in my sandals. You don't say?"

Even in the dim lighting, Cosmo could see the boss roll his eyes. Cosmo hadn't expected a royal greeting. He also hadn't expected to be mocked by the event organizer. Rather than be goaded into a response, he followed Mr. Khan's blank-faced lead.

The boss stared back and forth between the two before shaking his head. "No need to get in a tizzy. I'll overlook this emotional outburst since we've worked together so long." The boss nodded toward Cosmo. "But as for this greenhorn, there's fighting and then there's fighting."

Mr. Khan spoke into another extended period of silence with a single word. "Indeed."

The boss snorted. "So you're telling me this kid knows how to fight. We both know that doesn't mean he can fight, or even that he will fight. Jumping jiminetty, man, all the gods can see he isn't very big. And you said you wanted to match him up middleweight? What's to say one of those heavy schlubs doesn't just fall on him?"

The boss turned abruptly toward Cosmo. "You gonna break, kid? 'Cause I don't need some tribal boy coming into my barn just to break. It's bad for business, and I like my business to be good. Not bad. Snails! Aren't you gonna say something? You understand English don't you? 'Cause I'm afraid I don't speak Manipuri or whatever crazy dialect your mother tongue may be."

The man continued to mumble more to himself than to Cosmo. "Great horn spoon if those Naga Hills didn't end up being a Pandora's box of epic proportion—"

Having remained quiet as long as he could tolerate, Cosmo cut off the man's ramblings. "I've experienced much worse than fat men falling on me, and I've yet to break." In a combination of anger and dramatic flare, Cosmo flung off his gi. He turned to reveal the scars criss-crossing his back. The larger ones would be visible even in the dim lighting.

The boss drummed his fingers on his desk. "I see, a real warrior type. Still fighting the good fight and all. Well then," he scrutinized Cosmo anew, "don't go killing anybody—at least not on purpose. You stick to that and you're welcome in my barn, Mr. Cosmo Warrior."

The boss scratched his chin. "Maybe I'll even heed Mr. Khan's glowing endorsement and break my own rule by betting on a newbie. Now out with the both of you."

Cosmo didn't wait for Khan's lead this time. Without a word, he turned and left the cramped room. Eyes wide open, he understood the type of performance expected of him. And he understood the type of man who lusted for it.

Perhaps they would snigger at him for maintaining ideals. But Cosmo was above them and their filthy fight club. He would profit them, take his cut, and use the money to graduate from university. It was that simple.

Fight Culture and Opportunity

COSMO CAUGHT HIS OPPONENT'S leg. The attack had been sloppy at best. All the same, Cosmo had to respect the man's sheer size and strength. If he let himself get too close, the result could be cracked ribs or worse.

Cosmo spun the man to the side. Using his opponent's girth to block the referee's field of view, Cosmo delivered a punch to the man's groin. He followed it with one to the throat.

Before anyone could object, Cosmo swept the man's remaining leg. Driving him to the mat, he placed a knee in the man's chest and a choke on his already damaged larynx.

The fall knocked out his opponent's breath. After a few seconds of choking him, it became evident the man wasn't about to get up. The referee interceded and Cosmo relented. A dozen fights, a dozen wins.

The gathering of Indian businessmen, this time in a factory normally used to fabricate nylon feed sacks, cheered and hissed. Despite Cosmo's winning record, many continued to bet against the Naga warrior. Their racism clouded their judgment.

Some fights were uglier than others. Today he'd suffered only minor bruises, making it a good win. The referee rose from the mat after finishing the ten count. He whisked to Cosmo's side and raised his hand in victory. Unable to rise on his own, Cosmo's opponent accepted a helping hand.

Cosmo used the immediate business that followed every fight as his chance to slip from the ring and disappear into the makeshift dressing rooms converted out of conference rooms. Before he reached the hall leading from the factory floor, a hand reached for his shoulder.

He caught the hand and bent the wrist to the point of breaking.

A large Indian dressed in a suit dipped his shoulder and danced in the direction Cosmo steered him. The man gasped, "My boss just wants a moment of your time."

At once Cosmo understood the situation. This man was hired muscle, the kind of hired muscle paid well enough to dress in a suit nicer than anything Cosmo had ever thought of owning. He dropped the man's hand and stepped back. "Apologies. I thought perhaps someone was unhappy with my performance."

The hired muscle stopped short of rubbing his sore wrist. "My fault." His angry look didn't match his verbal concession. "As I was saying, my boss would like a word."

Cosmo raised a brow. "Oh?"

"For a proposition."

Cosmo hummed with heightened anticipation and alarm simultaneously. So far he'd steered clear of the affairs of those who attended the prizefights. He knew they included some of India's most nefarious sorts—dangerous people, connected people, rich people.

He hesitated. Delhi was supposed to be a new chapter in his life, a second chance. He was fighting for Jesus now, not for personal gain or selfish vindication.

On the other hand, he could use the additional money to do good. He could use the money to help the deserving poor create sustainable jobs. Plus, an outright rejection of the offer would carry risks of its own. Powerful people weren't fond of being snubbed, and Cosmo didn't even know who he'd be snubbing.

In the end, Cosmo simply nodded.

"Good. Clean yourself up. At your leisure meet me in the rug store on the corner. You'll be back in time to collect your winnings." The muscle suit strode away.

Cosmo continued toward the conference room where he'd left his street clothes in a plastic sack. His mind was abuzz with the mystery proposition—welcome and unwanted at the same time. The fact the muscle had mentioned Cosmo come 'at his leisure' indicated the sophistication of the matter. He knew the phrase meant he better not keep the boss waiting, but without having to state the obvious.

Above all else, Cosmo's response would need to be graceful. Like always, he'd step lightly around enemies of great position and power while testing where the opportunity could lead. As with all private jobs, this one would most likely be a matter of striving to gain loyalty without surrendering it.

In the end, he would allow the job to flow around him much the same way a rock anchored itself in the current of a polluted river. Whatever the job required of him in passing, he would remain rooted firmly in place long afterward.

Conflicts of Interest

KACHUI SOUNDED ANXIOUS AND rushed as he spoke.

Cosmo pressed his ear tightly to the telephone receiver in their shared dorm room. He didn't need to ask. He already knew the answer. Out of habit, he asked anyway. "Which is it this time?"

"Don't be smart, cousin. I'm sure you've heard rumors that party representatives are coming to campus."

"Rumors, yes."

"I promise you, they're true, and the Naga aren't the only ones who've heard."

"So you're saying the purpose of your invite is a fight, not a social?"

Kachui swore under his breath. "I'm saying unless you want two of our brightest leaders to be arrested—"

"Or killed," Cosmo interrupted.

"Then get to the cafe on Ring Road before the authorities do."

"I'm coming." Cosmo hung up. It took all his impulse control not to swear out loud. This was exactly the type of outside favor his employers had cautioned him against. Continuing his matches in the fight club provided no conflict of interest. The bosses gained added enjoyment from pitting their best men against each other for increased stakes.

Publicly intervening in a violent showdown between the Naga Student Union and student loyalists could land him in real trouble with both the government and his bosses. But Kachui and the others were his people, not self-aggrandizing Indian thugs. His employers paid him to perform a service. That was that. Cosmo knew where his loyalties laid.

Wearing sneakers, slacks and a long-sleeved shirt, he took the stairs a landing at a time. In less than twenty seconds he'd exited the student dorm complex and bolted toward Ring Road, north of campus. The Naga students frequented a cafe there. It had been stupid of them to choose such an obvious meeting spot.

Two minutes later, Cosmo sprinted into the cramped alley immediately behind the cafe. His sudden presence caught a clump of student loyalists off guard and in the process of lighting each other's cigarettes.

Leaning heavily on the element of surprise, Cosmo smashed the only camera he saw with a quick kick. He followed with a palm strike to the shocked student's nose. The blood spatter created further panic.

Snagging another student by the arm, Cosmo flung him into a third. Both of them crashed into a pallet stacked high with garbage. The rest of the group scattered.

Cosmo broke off the fight and kicked open the service door to the cafe. In the kitchen, he found a grateful Kachui.

"Thank God." Kachui gestured for three others to follow him and Cosmo out the back. "Did anyone recognize you?"

"I doubt it."

Kachui crammed into the service hall behind Cosmo. "If they're able to take pictures, or even gather names—"

"I smashed the only camera I saw. We're wasting time. I'll clear a hole. You lead the others." Cosmo burst back into the alley. None of the student spies loyal to the government had returned, but he could hear a gathering ruckus in front of the cafe. "Go."

Cosmo shielded his cousin and the others from any potential camera shots as they fled toward campus. He had instantly recognized those gathered under his cousin's care but avoided eye contact for the anonymity of everyone involved. This was not his business. He was a student, not a revolutionary.

Before the student loyalists had a chance to identify him, Cosmo followed Kachui's retreat. He'd ensure the visitors cleared campus and avoided arrest or worse. But that was it.

Anyone associated with the revolutionaries was regarded as an enemy combatant or terrorist. While the local police were a joke, certain government authorities were not to be taken lightly. There had been rumors of a ceasefire and peace talks between the government of India and the Naga. But they were merely rumors. Even if they became reality, Cosmo doubted the Indians were capable of honoring any such process.

Cosmo shook political thoughts out of his mind as he checked over his shoulder for pursuers. He saw no one. Ahead, he caught a glimpse of Kachui and the others ducking into a fenced off maintenance area. He slowed to a walk and relaxed his breathing.

Kachui and the two revolutionary party delegates had been accompanied by another Naga student. Cosmo knew him. He worked as a groundskeeper on campus. Sure enough, a minute later a maintenance truck pulled out of the garage and headed calmly off campus. Two students sat in the front—Kachui in the passenger seat. A canvas tarp covered the truck bed.

Whistling, Cosmo strolled casually toward his dorm as if on a study break. And why not? He had been studying for his second year exams before Kachui had imposed his cause into Cosmo's life yet again.

Between his secrets and his cousin's—Cosmo shook his head. They'd gotten lucky this time. With a little expert juggling, none of the balls had been dropped. A year left in his studies, Cosmo feared the luck wouldn't hold.

Culture: Politics and the Dalits

IT'S LITTLE WONDER THE Naga did not and still do not perceive joining the Republic of India as desirable. While the concept of "untouchability" was outlawed within the Indian constitution, popular opinion and discrimination were not. The Dalits continue to suffer in modern India. The technical jargon of India's constitution refers to these people as Scheduled Castes and Scheduled Tribes (some 16% and 8% of the population respectively).

The Naga fit into the category of Scheduled Tribe. Within Indian society and Indian governance, Nagas would instantly be lumped into the lower 25% of the population. They are below caste.

Adding to the discrimination, Nagas typically have smaller eyes. Their ethnicity is Mongoloid, and they're vastly agrarian. India is among the most diverse countries in the world. As is always the case, this diversity carries prejudice with it. While not uniformly hated or discriminated against, there is little within Indian society which appeals to Nagas.

The majority of Naga society has long been more egalitarian than the caste system of India. This basic cultural incompatibility drew Cosmo Zimik's attention soon after he arrived in Delhi. At first, it confused and astounded him that such a large percentage of the Indian population could be contained and oppressed by so few in power.

Some say including the Scheduled Castes and Scheduled Tribes with the Other Backward Classes encompasses over half the population of India. At the same time, the priestly or Brahmin caste consists of approximately 5%.

With corruption and nepotism running rampant through all branches of government and law enforcement, Cosmo marveled that the system worked at all. After spending two years studying Indian bureaucracy and politics, participating in multiple student organizations, and saturating himself in all aspects of Indian society, he grew convinced the Dalits were the lynchpin in reforming the Indian government.

Due to their forced association since 1954, many Nagas had come to sympathize with the Dalits of India. At twenty-one years of age, Cosmo believed the kinship of suffering shared between India's non-casted, lowest rung of society and the Naga could evolve into a political partnership in their mutual struggle for self-determination.

He also believed that if these oppressed people could manage two victories—one over fear and one over poverty—they would rise to grasp the power the Indian constitution technically provided for them while practically withholding from them. The route to these victories would not be through violence, but instead through self-sustaining economic development. Then, and only then, things would really change.

For the most part, Cosmo kept his theories to himself. But his unique experience and elite skills never allowed him to remain in the shadows for long. Near the end of his second year of studies, Cosmo was approached by Naga revolutionaries. They wanted to hear what he had to say about the Dalits. After his exams, he traveled to the jungles of northeast India for a meeting.

A Meeting in the Jungle

COSMO STARED OVERHEAD AT the small patch of clouds visible through the jungle canopy. The distant buzz of a Jeep lapped at his ears as if riding on ripples of humidity. A macaw stretched out its wings and lifted from its perch. With three powerful strokes, it disappeared through the gap in the canopy.

The freedom of flight washed over Cosmo. He felt the imagery in his bones. His people would never fly as part of India. They had been unjustly invaded by hostile forces infinitely larger than their own. The Naga had been at war with this Goliath for nearly half a century, and yet they had not bowed their neck or bent their knee.

He knew they would never surrender. How can a people who have never been conquered, a people who view each other as equals, settle for anything less than freedom and equality?

Gradually the buzz of the Jeep grew into the growl of half a dozen Jeeps. Cosmo sat, legs crossed, his sword in his lap. It was the least alert posture within his martial arts training.

To squat or to recline on one's knees enabled the warrior to quickly leap to his feet and draw his sword. To sit cross-legged meant total trust in the safety of one's surroundings. It indicated this meeting was to be between family.

As the Jeeps grew loud enough to overpower the natural sounds of the jungle, Cosmo closed his eyes and focused on teasing the more subtle sounds out of hiding. The nearby river remained the loudest jungle voice. A monkey screeched—the only large animal undeterred by so much human activity.

Then, one by one, the Jeeps skid to a sudden stop and killed their engines. After the last one died, Cosmo heard the creaks and pops of the cooling vehicles. He opened his eyes. He recognized one of the men from the cafe on Ring Road in Delhi.

This was a man of action. The man's movements revealed as much. Cosmo connected with him at an elementary level. He felt honored to share such company. Perhaps these men were part of the solution for bringing freedom to the Naga. Cosmo wondered if God had preserved his life for this reason.

To Cosmo's surprise, the meeting began with tea, even in the midst of the jungle. His hosts explained that such subtleties set them apart from the animals. They drank politely, but quickly. Without further delay, they transitioned to the business at hand.

The questions were simple and broad, offered to encourage Cosmo to share his thoughts in their entirety. While he spoke, the Naga revolutionaries listened. For two hours, Cosmo addressed their increasingly detailed inquiries until the conversation came to a sudden stop.

The lead delegate rose from the jungle floor and stretched. The rest followed, as did Cosmo. The troops revered their leader, giving him their highest regard. Cosmo did not doubt the men would offer their lives to save the man they served.

"Thank you for your words." The man bowed slightly.

Cosmo bowed lower.

"You have surprising wisdom and cunning insight for such a young warrior. You would make a valuable addition to the party."

Cosmo shuddered. He had not anticipated such an unfettered invitation. A significant part of him leaped at the thought. But as he breathed deeply, he sensed the inflation of his pride. He did not want to make such an important decision based on an emotional response to flattery.

Plus, his studies had convinced him a direct military approach would never succeed against India. The last two years in Delhi had led him further from the jungle warrior of his adolescence.

"I am honored to be considered worthy." Cosmo finally rose from his bowed position. "But such an important invitation would be disparaged by a quick response."

The man nodded. "The invitation is an open one. Thank you for your efforts to meet us for this short time." He motioned to the others. "Speaking of time, we've been still for too long."

With an economy of movement learned only through years of jungle combat, the soldiers mounted their vehicles and disappeared within seconds, save for the dissipating mechanical growl of their Jeeps.

Cosmo remained in place until the growl faded to a mosquito buzz. Finally, in ripples, it disappeared all together. He pulled a hunk of smoked pork from his pocket and turned toward the village where he grew up.

The time was just past noon. If he hurried, he would arrive at his parents' door before dark—assuming he didn't encounter the need to draw the sword dangling from his belt.

With each stride, the sword slapped lightly against his thigh, comforting him. The jungle comforted him. The thought of home comforted him.

While the decision before him was an important one, he would not be anxious over making it. Either way, opportunity awaited.

A Home Without Snakes

EN ROUTE TO HIS home village, Cosmo stopped at a crossroads to buy fresh food for dinner. Twenty minutes later, he boarded a bus with a plastic sack full of cabbage, eggs, pork and a bunch of bananas. He hadn't considered the difficulty of helping his parents without drawing attention to the easy money he'd been making.

He relaxed as the bus jostled along the dirt road. His parents knew nothing about city life. It wouldn't be hard to convince them he'd earned the money from martial arts tournaments, or for offering private lessons. And he'd be telling a partial truth.

An hour later, he stepped off the bus and strode across the village to his parents' hut—to the hut he'd grown up in. It'd only been a year since he'd been home. Each year's passing increased the burden he felt when he returned.

No one should be subject to the poverty he had grown up with, and yet that same poverty strangled his village the same as a thousand others. If anything, its grip strengthened each year. And if poverty made people desperate, oppression made them mean. Cosmo wanted so much more for the Nagas.

"Son!" Cosmo's mother dropped her hoe and straightened her back before hurrying to greet him.

Cosmo embraced her. Having been taller than her since his teens, he now stood a head higher. "You're shrinking."

"You're still growing." She smiled up at him.

Cosmo shifted the plastic sack from one hand to the other.

"You brought something?"

He escorted her to the front door and opened it for her. "I wanted to help out with dinner. It's nothing special."

His mother flowed gracefully toward the stove where the fire had already been lit. "Oh?"

Cosmo picked up on the hidden question in her one word comment. "I'll tell you all about life in Delhi later, after dinner." He paused. "I know you and father don't like me fighting, but there are tournaments in the city, and lots of Indians anxious to learn Thaing." Finally he shrugged. "I'm good at it."

His mother patted the preparatory table next to the stove. "I believe you. Now why don't you show me what you bought so I can cook it, and we can eat." She turned toward him suddenly when he set the bag down. "It's not snakes, is it?"

They both laughed. "You're never going to let that one go, are you?"

She shivered as she hefted the pork from the bag. "I hate snakes."

A Father's Warning

"GOD HAS TOLD ME, son, in no uncertain terms." Cosmo's father leaned forward. Resting his elbows on the table, he held his teacup in front of his face and blew across it. "He will not use the Revolutionary Party to bring freedom to our people. If you join them, you will be throwing away the talents God has trusted in you."

"What about Aring?" Cosmo stared at the table.

"I have given my oldest son the same warning." Cosmo's father squeezed his wife's hand as the two of them exchanged a grieved look. "He has chosen not to heed it."

Cosmo shook his head. "And Muivah? It's said he's a godly man. Why wouldn't God share the same words with him?"

Cosmo's father nodded. "Indeed, I believe Muivah to be a godly as well as a goodly man. I don't know, son, God may have a role for him yet."

"Have you heard our cousin's stories?" Cosmo asked.

"Yes." His father sipped his tea. "I'm assuming you mean the story of Muivah surviving the hail of gunfire from half a dozen helicopters—how the bullets could not harm him." He sipped again. "I have no reason to doubt it's truth. But even King Saul was God's anointed."

Cosmo looked into his father's eyes. "I don't understand."

"Have you still not studied the whole of King David's story?" He rested his tea on the table. "Bah. Too much science and too little Scripture. Saul was king of the Hebrews before David, before there was a kingdom to be king over. He was a mighty man, a man of action, the people's king. But David—he answered to God. You remember the story of Goliath?"

Cosmo nodded. He had in fact reread the story recently.

His father closed his eyes and winced, as if reliving an old injury. "Your oldest brother believes humility to be synonymous with weakness, therefore he misunderstands the critical truth in the Goliath story. He sees it as a story of courage and pride in the face of daunting challenge."

"Is he wrong?" Cosmo wouldn't have simplified in the same manner, but he couldn't see any clear fault in the summary.

"Perhaps not wrong, but wrongly focused." His father grinned as he picked up his tea and gulped it. Cosmo's father warmed to his subject, even while his tea cooled. He enjoyed the fact there was still a thing or two he could teach the scholar in the family.

"David defeated Goliath because he relied on God's might rather than his own. The boy, David, displayed a personal humility in conjunction with a divine pride. It is a rare leader who understands the balance. You see, humility can open us up to a power infinitely greater than our own."

His father's teaching sparked a question Cosmo hadn't been able to resolve during his study of the passage. "And when David refused Saul's personal armor—"

"He refused traditional military wisdom, choosing instead the weapon of a shepherd."

"The shepherd king." Cosmo finished his father's thought as the answer to his question clicked in his brain. "So it was not a military solution to the problem at all, but a spiritual one."

"Repentance before revolution." His father nodded. "Our people will find deliverance only if they look to the Lord to deliver them. But they are like sheep without a shepherd."

Cosmo sensed the wisdom of his father's words. As excited as he'd been in the jungle when speaking with the delegates of the Revolutionary Party, an even deeper resonance churned inside him as his father spoke of the power unleashed by humility. "With prideful hearts, the Naga cannot defeat the Indians." Cosmo tested the validity of the idea by speaking it aloud.

"Mahatma Gandhi understood the teaching as well as anyone, even if he did not understand the source. You cannot seize humility. You cannot boast of its conquest. And you cannot obtain true humility while grasping any form of worldly success. It must be received with empty hands."

Cosmo shivered. There it was again. Something vague and hungry tugged at the back of his awareness. It passed before he could identify it. To focus himself he repeated his father's words from earlier. "Repentance before revolution."

His father nodded. "When we confront India with personal humility and divine pride, God will deliver us on that day, even if our deliverance comes, as it did for Gandhi, at great personal cost."

A Rainy Day

THE RAIN ENVELOPED THE cricket field and filled the air to the point of laboring Cosmo's every breath. It seemed his third year at university had thus far been one solid rainstorm. He scooped a sodden newspaper from a puddle and used it to shield the downpour from his face. Not a single other soul had braved the deluge to join him for a workout.

No wonder. Rain was one thing. This was a bit extreme, even for Cosmo. Convinced no one else would show, he decided to take the day off as well. The time was after 6:00pm. Due to the torrential rain, daylight had already transitioned to night.

He headed toward his dorm at a jog. Along the way, he decided he better take a pit stop behind the supply shed to relieve himself. Before he had the opportunity, a muffled scream chilled him to the bone. It was a woman's scream—the sort of scream that spoke of a person's worst fears.

Fueled by an adrenaline surge, Cosmo rounded the shed and kicked in the corrugated metal door. What he saw caused him pause. Even suspecting the worst hadn't prepared him for the presence of five men clumped around a solitary woman half stripped of her clothing.

"Bugger off!" One of the men attempted to slam the door shut.

Cosmo propped it open with his foot. The impact jarred him from his shock. Flowing forward, he slammed his forearm into the nose and cheek of the man who had spoke. At the same time, he used his other hand to jab a second man in the solar plexus.

Another attempted to lift himself off of the woman. Helping him, Cosmo planted a foot in the man's side. Caught in his own zipper, the man howled as he crashed into a wall of garden tools.

The rest of Cosmo's movements were dictated by his attackers. As each attempted to land a punch or a hold, he countered while dealing as much damage as he could without slowing down or obsessing with any single foe. In a matter of seconds the outcome had been determined in his favor.

Seconds after that, none of the five were able to rise.

Cowering next to a fifty-gallon drum, the woman struggled to cover herself with her remaining clothing. Soaking wet, shivering and smeared with mud, she shielded her face.

Cosmo realized she was approximately his own age. Methodically, he checked each of the five attackers, ensuring they'd be no more trouble. He knelt beside the man who had yelled at him, presumably the ringleader, and spoke into his ear loud enough to be heard over the chorus of rain thundering against the tin roof. "I know your faces. If you try anything like this again, next time you won't get off so easy."

The man grunted. His one good eye roved wildly in his head, unable to focus.

Cosmo gathered the girl's remaining clothes and draped them over her.

She flinched at the contact, but quickly dressed herself as well as she could.

Cosmo shuffled toward the door with his back turned. "I'm sorry for what has happened to you. I know it doesn't undo what has been done, but at least you won't have to worry about these monsters again." Cosmo waited several seconds. All he heard was the rain.

He wondered if he should leave. He didn't want to make the matter worse. At the same time, he wanted to see it through. "I can go now, if you—"

"Thank you for saving me."

Slowly, Cosmo turned to face her. Her clothes were muddy and slightly torn, but not indecent. The look in her eyes was one of shock. Cosmo knew she wouldn't get home on her own. "Do you live on campus?"

She shook her head.

"Let me help you to a rickshaw."

She stared at him, unmoving. Then, as if remembering the event anew, she burst into tears.

"Here." Cosmo gently escorted her through the tangled mess of maintenance equipment, lawn tools and groaning perverts. Outside the supply shed, the rain seemed quiet in comparison.

Cosmo did his best to stabilize the girl without violating her space or spooking her further. To his surprise, she clung to him, trusting him completely to guide her to safety. It took only a few minutes to reach the edge of campus and locate an autowallah who looked trustworthy. While paying the driver in advance, Cosmo stared at him with enough malice to ensure he remained on his best behavior.

He turned to the girl. "You'll be alright from here?"

She nodded. "My apartment's not far." The color had returned to her face. She smiled. "Thank you, really. You stopped them before anything terrible could happen."

"I'm just glad I came along when I did." Cosmo straightened and tapped the roof of the rickshaw.

The driver pulled away from the curb.

The girl suddenly yelled over the combined noise of the rain and traffic. "What's your name?"

As the merging rickshaw accelerated, he yelled after it. "Cosmo."

Entrepreneurialism

COSMO PLACED THE POT of leftover rice on the single burner cooktop and topped it off with milk. He would have preferred a sausage, but there wasn't a scrap of meat in the dorm. All he discovered while scrounging through the cupboard was a small tin of ground cinnamon. He couldn't think of who had bought it, or how long ago. Pemi must have tried to cook for a girl.

"Late night?"

Cosmo glanced up.

His cousin, Kachui, stood at his bedroom door. He rubbed his eyes.

"I'm sorry if I woke you."

Kachui waved off the apology and headed for the toilet. "Since when do you get in later than Pemi on a Saturday night?"

"I missed the bus, that's all." Cosmo found a wooden spoon on the counter and held it up for inspection before using it to stir the rice. In fact, he had ridden the bus to a private hospital where he'd received half a dozen stitches.

They had made him wait in the lobby so long, he'd been forced to walk most of the way home before flagging down an auto rickshaw to take him the rest of the way. The prizefight had been a victory, but the most painful victory of his third year at university.

Kachui snorted at the lame cover story.

"Since you're up, you might as well turn on the lights."

"Don't rush me." Kachui disappeared into the cramped

bathroom. After emerging, he flipped on the lights. "Didn't you miss the bus last weekend too? Or was it the weekend before that?"

Cosmo kept his back toward his cousin while testing the consistency of the rice.

"You really should buy yourself a watch. Maybe then you wouldn't miss so many buses on your way home from wherever you're fighting to earn all your mysterious extra income."

Cosmo set down the spoon and sighed. "It's that obvious?"

Kachui plopped onto the couch. "You're talented, cousin. You'd be stupid not to take advantage of that."

"Really?" Cosmo turned to face his cousin for the first time.

Kachui raised a brow when he spotted the stitches above his cousin's left eye. Then he shrugged. "Most of us are gonna end up farming or teaching if we're lucky. Those with an able body pedal a rickshaw or porter someone else's junk. You've got skills that are in demand."

Cosmo returned to stirring his rice. Life would be easier now that his cousin knew of his fighting, but a part of him wished Kachui hadn't approved so readily. He could have at least shown more surprise.

Had Cosmo's reputation become so smudged that the revelation of his association with Delhi's seamy fight culture warranted nothing more than a raised brow? Did he appear a thug to his fellow classmates?

Kachui continued. "The only thing that frustrates me, is that while you're willing to beat up Indians for money, you're unwilling to fight for the cause of our people."

Cosmo should have seen it coming. He removed the rice and turned off the burner. "Cinnamon?"

"Sure."

Cosmo sprinkled the ground cinnamon liberally over the rice. After stirring it in, he split the rice between two bowls and left the pot in the sink. "There's more than one way to fight." He handed one of the bowls to his cousin.

Kachui blew across his bowl. "You can't do both at once?"

"As a matter of fact, I can't."

"Or you won't."

Cosmo opened the blinds. The eastward view revealed an obstructed skyline transitioning from steely grey to subtle shades of pink and orange. He swallowed a bite of rice. "You know my ideas about the Dalits?"

"Of course."

"You yourself admitted that most of us will be lucky to teach or perhaps farm."

Kachui nodded while spooning in his breakfast.

"It's our third year. I plan on getting my certificate in May. I've given up on the dream of a government position. The Indian government is so corrupt and driven by nepotism—"

"No argument there."

"But private business is growing," Cosmo said.

"Not very much."

"Maybe so, but there's promise in being an entrepreneur." Cosmo scooped in a spoon of rice.

"And the Dalits? What promise is there for them?" Kachui asked. "They are the lowest caste and the poorest class in all of India."

"They've got the most to gain and the least to lose."

"So you're going to fight for the Dalits instead of the Naga?"

Cosmo scraped milk from his chin with his spoon. "We're one and the same."

Kachui snorted. "Now who's talking like an Indian?"

"That's exactly the point. To the Indians, we're all lower than scum. As long as they keep the scum divided into small, manageable camps, we're no threat to the minority in power. In government, power makes the rules. In business, money makes the rules."

"And you've recently gotten a taste for money."

Kachui's words stung. He made Cosmo's ambitions sound selfish and driven by simple greed. "Even a small business could change a dozen lives for the better. A larger vision of economic sustainability could change hundreds of thousands. Our culture could be healed. Or have you forgotten what it was like to be hungry, and to be helpless to do anything about it?"

"At least I haven't forgotten about our people."

Cosmo stomped into the kitchen and clanked his bowl into the sink, nearly breaking it. "I've bailed you and your brothers out of trouble so many times—"

Kachui interrupted. "I thought maybe this term would be different, after your trip home last summer."

Cosmo remembered his father's words from a few months earlier, *repentance before revolution.*

"Instead you've been even less involved than before. And you're gone fighting every Saturday. You're always fighting."

Cosmo opened his mouth to speak.

Kachui cut him off. "Sorry. I never meant to pick a fight. I just miss hanging out with you, that's all. I know the others do too. You barely even make time to see Priya anymore.

Cosmo breathed deeply. The way he'd met Priya, saving her from would-be rapists, had been fortuitous indeed. He had thought about inviting her to a church service later that morning. "You think she'll like the stitches?"

Kachui smiled. "She'll love them."

"Maybe we could all head to church together."

"Sure thing, cousin." Kachui stood and headed for the kitchen. "As long as you're buying lunch afterward. Maybe some of that lamb korma you've been raving about."

"Lamb?"

"Or chicken." Kachui placed his bowl in the sink. "I'm not picky."

Battlefield

AS THE TERM ROUNDED out and the autumn of Cosmo's third year of university transitioned into winter, the knowledge of Cosmo's prizefighting spread. If anything, the revelation increased his standing with his fellow students rather than hurt it. Enrollment in his Thaing class doubled, as did the students' dedication.

On a cool December afternoon, Cosmo led his class through an active regimen of kicks and punches before pairing them off to spar. Over the last year, he'd recognized improvement in his students as well as his teaching. The less his instruction focused on the need to impart his skills, and the more it focused on bringing out his students' abilities, the more fulfilling teaching became.

Besides, his reputation had spread so far he felt the need to play down his talent rather than highlight it. He glanced at his new watch to confirm what he already knew—the time had come to dismiss the class. "That's good for today."

A few of the sparring partners broke off instantly. Several others continued. As Cosmo collected his mat, one of the more talented male students approached him.

"Um, teacher?"

"Yes?" They exchanged bows.

"I hope this doesn't come across wrong, but, uh…"

"Go ahead." Cosmo nudged him.

"I was wondering if I could, this weekend…um, if I could watch you fight."

Cosmo scratched the back of his neck. No one had openly asked him to attend a fight. Obviously this eager student didn't understand how they worked. Then again, Cosmo hadn't understood until he'd experienced it firsthand. "I'm sorry, it doesn't work that way."

"Oh, I'm sorry." The student bowed again. "I didn't mean—"

Cosmo smiled. "No offense taken. It's just that, well, the events aren't open to the general public. And I'm not in a position to make invitations."

"I understand."

Over the student's shoulder Cosmo watched a large group of athletes assemble on the opposite side of the field. "You're talented and disciplined. Keep working. Fight clubs aren't for everyone."

Dejected, the student bowed a final time and hurried off.

Cosmo glanced a second time across the cricket field. The group of thirty plus people spread into formation and unfurled flags—Hindu militants. Cosmo bristled. Class having ended, there was no need to fight over the field. Still, the arrogance of the Hindus offended him.

As the group marched toward Cosmo, he recognized their leader—a young man named Kumar. Cosmo had butted heads with the hot-tempered Indian on a dozen occasions. The last time, Cosmo's class had been smaller and less skilled. This time he'd already dismissed them.

When Cosmo turned around, he discovered over a dozen of his students had lingered. Identifying his best three students and a handful more with promise, he deemed their force sufficient. The students shifted uncomfortably. He gave the thumbs up and motioned for them to stay put rather than clump up behind him.

As the militants drew close, Cosmo turned his attention to Kumar. A runt even smaller than Cosmo, Kumar made up for his size with scrap and determination. He may not have been a true believer, but he took joy in pushing people around. And he was disciplined.

The cricket squad and the wrestling team could no longer intimidate Cosmo's class. All that remained was to teach Kumar's militants a lesson. Then, Cosmo would dominate the most desired field during the most sought after time of the day.

Five meters away, Kumar raised his hand. The entire troop stopped on cue.

Cosmo thought it funny. "I like your socks."

Kumar refused to look down at his knee high socks colored gold and red to match the flags they carried. A deity of some sort emblazoned the banners, but there wasn't enough breeze to unfurl them.

Cosmo couldn't identify the character and didn't care to.

"We've used this field longer than you, and we're claiming the space. So back off." Kumar said.

Cosmo shrugged. "It's a good thing you waited for half my class to leave."

"I saw them run away when we arrived. Now you can do the same."

Without turning around, Cosmo motioned a handful of his students to his right. As he did so, he scooped his toes beneath a dummy knife he'd brought for training purposes. "This way will be more embarrassing for you when you lose."

Kumar gave the signal to advance.

Cosmo popped the heavy rubber knife into the air and caught it in a single motion.

Kumar hesitated a split second at the appearance of the knife.

Cosmo took full advantage. Slashing the dummy knife across Kumar's chest, Cosmo spun and leapt. As Kumar stumbled backward, Cosmo caught him in the side of the head with his knee and threw him to the ground.

Maintaining his balance, Cosmo attacked the left side of the Hindu formation using Burmese Thaing. Despite the flimsy nature of the dummy knife, Thaing adapted well to street fighting, especially when facing multiple opponents. In this case, he bruised people instead of cutting them.

The last few weeks of class had focused on adapting traditional martial arts for fighting in the streets. This would be a perfect opportunity for his students to gain real life application. When the rules changed, technique had to follow. Otherwise a black belt meant nothing in the real world. Rule one: attack fast and constantly engage the next fighter.

Always keep moving.

Cosmo flashed in circular patterns, striking his attackers with both fist and foot. Occasionally, situation demanded he use a knee or his head. In general, he tried to keep the militants at arms' length.

Their numbers dwindled until he was fighting only one or two at a time. Cosmo remained on the attack. Then, with a final elbow and forearm to a face, the fight ended. From beginning to end, it had taken maybe two minutes.

Cosmo checked a final time to ensure none of the militants planned on getting up. Then he scanned his class—four plus himself had remained in the fight. "Well done." He bowed. They did the same. "Help the others. We all fought well today."

One of his students had been dazed badly enough to need assistance off the field. The others were able to walk off under their own power. No one would need medical attention. At least, none of his students would.

Cosmo stayed behind to collect his mat and duffle. He waited for Kumar to struggle to his feet before turning to go. "Good try, my friend. Maybe next time you should bring different flags. But keep the socks. Those I like."

The Devil Collects Twice

COSMO POUNDED THE PUNCHING bag twenty-five times with his right before switching to his left. Backing up a step, he counted twenty-five high kicks with each foot and then started the whole cycle over again for the fifth time.

Usually during the fourth rotation he reached a level of clearheadedness that benefitted his studies and relationships—fit body, sharp mind. Today he simply felt tired. Before he could finish the fifth cycle, a coughing fit seized him.

He leaned on the punching bag and labored to catch his breath. A shooting pain in his lower back intensified with each cough. Maybe he'd been pushing himself too hard with final exams only a week away. Somehow, exams felt empty and important at the same time.

He closed his eyes through another bout of coughing.

Everything his classmates strove for felt empty. Their degrees weren't going to land them the cushy government jobs they dreamed of. Cosmo remained convinced of the private sector's promise. No certificate of graduation was needed to be your own boss.

But he had started university, and that meant he would finish. He would finish strong so no one would doubt his ability. Finally, he managed to draw a full breath without coughing.

He opened his eyes. Someone had spattered blood on the punching bag and carelessly failed to clean it up. Grimacing, he stretched his back and trotted toward the hamper full of gym rags. When he reached for one, he realized his hands were covered with blood as well.

He wiped his chin and came away with more. Then the coughing started in earnest. By the time Cosmo staggered through the gym door, he'd soaked the gym rag with bright, red blood, and his back was forcing him to limp.

At first, the rickshaw driver baulked at giving Cosmo a ride. It wasn't every day a man soaked in sweat and coughing up blood solicited one's services. Growling through his teeth, Cosmo asked to be taken to the same private hospital that had stitched him up the previous year.

Rather than test Cosmo's resilience, the driver relented.

The hospital wasn't far. Cosmo tumbled from the cycle rickshaw before it skidded to a stop. Forgetting to pay, he picked himself up and limped through the front doors.

On seeing the amount of blood dripping from the rag pressed to Cosmo's face, the attendant admitted him immediately. Minutes later, Cosmo was lying on a doctor's table with a fresh towel.

Without saying much, and asking nothing, the doctor smeared an ointment in and around Cosmo's nose. After a half hour, the coughing and bleeding slowed to intermittent fits.

Using a wheelchair, a nurse escorted Cosmo to a room shared by three other patients. Cosmo wanted to ask how much it would cost him to even sit down in such a room. But the staff had ignored his previous questions, so he held his tongue.

A few hours later, the doctor showed up with a clipboard and a pen and a bunch of questions. "Are you active?"

"Do you smoke or chew betel nuts?"

"What were you doing when the coughing began?"

The questions continued like this for several minutes with the doctor scrolling illegible notes before asking another. Looking up from his clipboard, the doctor asked a final question. This time he spoke more as a human than a machine of medical diagnosis. "Have you experienced any violent trauma in your past?"

Cosmo's breath caught in his throat. He swallowed. "Yes." He was pretty sure his scars revealed that much.

The doctor continued. "On a scale of one to ten, ten being quite life threatening—"

"Ten." Cosmo didn't wait for the doctor to finish.

The doctor nodded. "I see." He set his clipboard aside and rested his hands in his lap. "I can't be certain before seeing the results of an x-ray. I'd like to take a CT scan and run an MRI. But I believe it quite likely that your internal bleeding is the result of a previous injury. Your workout today only exacerbated a problem that has probably been building over the course of several months."

"Will it heal?"

"That depends on the injury. It hasn't healed on its own thus far." The doctor straightened. "An MRI and a CT scan will tell me much more, but they are expensive. Are you familiar with—"

"Magnetic Resonance Imaging and Computed Tomography. Yes, I understand the technology."

The doctor raised a brow.

"I'm a bio-chemistry student."

"Ah. Good for you. Then you'll understand that the scans will give me the ability to identify the exact nature of the bleeding and your back pain in order to determine a treatment."

Cosmo nodded. "I've got some money, but not much." He hadn't been fighting as often this year, and he didn't have much money laid aside for emergencies like this. He'd always assumed he could simply show up and fight when he needed more.

"I'll schedule the tests while the nurse gets you the paperwork." The doctor nodded toward the door. "Nurse."

"Yes, doctor." The nurse dutifully wheeled Cosmo out of the room in the wheelchair they had confined him to.

As she pushed him slowly down the hall, Cosmo watched the random pattern on the linoleum floor pass beneath. Cascading and broken flashes of the violent episode that nearly killed him rippled across his thoughts.

How had the doctor put it? *Life threatening violent trauma*—a fancy way of saying he had almost died. Lurking beneath Cosmo's fragmented mental state, a fear rose in his gut—his past was returning to finish the job.

PART 4

SECOND CHANCES

Stranded and Alone

THE FIRST DAY IN the hospital had been broken up by tests and scans. After a night of fitful sleep on the hospital bed, Cosmo woke up stiffer than ever. He tried to call Pemi and Kachui half a dozen times. No one answered.

After two full days in the hospital without a visitor, Cosmo called Priya. Like an angel, she appeared in the doorway of his hospital room. The lights in the hallway created a halo effect around her wild, black hair. She brought him his books along with some smuggled curry. They conversed politely for an hour before she apologized and excused herself for class.

Cosmo thanked her for coming.

As the whir of medical machinery replaced her presence, Cosmo felt emptier than he had before her visit. He hadn't been tempted to share his real feelings with her. While she was beautiful and kind, she was no kindred spirit. He had rescued her once, but she could not rescue him.

Over the next two days Cosmo attempted to pass the time by completing his exams. Without interruption from friend, family or doctor, the pain in his back served as his only distraction. One more week, if he could survive it, and he would cross the university finish line at the age of twenty-two. Even if he had to do so from a hospital bed—at the age of twenty-two.

He struggled to focus. He forced his mind to bungle through the process. The whole time, fear stalked him. Feelings of betrayal and abandonment filled the space that remained.

On his fourth night in the hospital, Cosmo lay awake in bed. He groaned and shifted in an effort to relieve the dull ache in his back. The medical staff had told him next to nothing about his condition. But he knew what was happening. His body was paying the price for a decade of arrogance and misdeeds.

A heart-monitoring device, connected to a patient sharing Cosmo's room, droned in the background. The man hadn't been conscious at any point during Cosmo's stay. His vitals hadn't changed at all. Cosmo shifted again. The bed next to him had been vacated the day before and remained empty. He was grateful for small mercies.

At 3:00am the hospital reached its lowest level of activity. Cosmo closed his eyes and tried to decipher each scattered sound. He bored of the game in minutes.

He tried to direct his anger at God, but couldn't. It made no rational sense to be angry at God or anyone other than himself. Cosmo knew of his choices when he made them. His current condition was the result—simple cause and effect.

In fact, the longer he lay awake, the more he felt only God remained by his side. His friends had abandoned him. Perhaps he had not always been the most attentive friend in return, but he had always been faithful. Ironic. After all the times he had consciously withheld his loyalty while achieving loyalty from others, the practice had come around to kick him in the back, hard.

Just before slipping off to sleep, Cosmo's thoughts landed at the base of his most primal fear. If his body was truly broken, what of him would remain?

The Bad News

"THE WORST INJURY IS to your spine, Mr. Zimik. It's probable the damage to your lung tissue will repair on its own over time. And honestly, the ruptured capillaries that caused your internal hemorrhaging remain mysterious. I've never seen anything quite like it. Suffice to say, that bleeding led to the awareness of your spinal injury."

"Which is?" Cosmo sat up in bed with difficulty. He sensed the doctor dancing around the bad news.

"Right. At some point in your past, several of your lumbar vertebrae suffered severe trauma, apparent today by the amount of scar tissue and resultant nerve damage. According to your own account, they miraculously healed on their own." The doctor frowned, revealing once again he believed very little of Cosmo's description of recovering from an accident.

He continued. "Despite the appearance of recovery, the scar tissue surrounding the injuries has not healed in the slightest. Quite the opposite. That scar tissue is putting pressure on your spine. To make matters worse, the disks between L3 and L4 and L4 and L5 are both herniated." The doctor indicated a section of the scan Cosmo held. "Truthfully, I'm shocked you can still walk without tremendous pain."

"I walked in here easily enough." Cosmo studied the results of the MRI rather than look the doctor in the eye.

"Another miracle, Mr. Zimik. But given your current nerve damage and the two herniated disks, I recommend immediate surgery."

"Surgery?" Cosmo's throat constricted. "What kind of surgery?"

"Without going into too much detail, I strongly recommend placing a series of six pins along each side of your spine to stabilize the region and prevent further nerve damage."

Cosmo closed his eyes. Nothing about what the doctor was saying seemed either acceptable or possible. Yet he knew it to be true. He also knew the word 'stabilize' meant a significant section of his back would no longer move. That meant martial arts would be impossible. "What kind of nerve damage?"

The doctor shrugged. "Paralysis. Remember, Mr. Zimik, I'm surprised you're not paralyzed already. While I can't guarantee the surgery will prevent all further nerve damage, it will greatly increase the likelihood."

"And without the surgery?"

The doctor took the scan from Cosmo and studied it afresh. He cleared his throat. "Based on the scan alone, I'd say you were already paralyzed from the waist down. Given your current condition, I don't know. At some point, sooner than later, you'll lose the ability to walk. Maybe six months from now."

Cosmo pinched his eyes shut. He had already been in the hospital for five days. He didn't want to stay a moment longer. He didn't have the money to pay the bills he'd already racked up, much less for complex surgery.

If he left the building, perhaps he could leave the knowledge of his injuries as well. Maybe the doctor was wrong. Maybe everything would be fine. After several seconds of silence, Cosmo addressed the doctor without opening his eyes. "Can I leave now?"

The doctor gasped, but quickly recovered. "I see." He ran his hand through his neatly combed hair. "I cannot in good conscious let you go today."

Cosmo wanted to argue.

"But," the doctor continued, "If you permit me to administer a pain and inflammation relieving injection into your spine, by tomorrow morning you should be in decent enough shape to be released with the aid of a wheelchair." He paused. "And attempt to enjoy the mobility you've got left."

Cosmo stared at the wall. "Fine. Let's do that."

After the doctor left the room, Cosmo counted to sixty before unplugging himself. He swung his legs off the bed and stood. The effort made his head spin. Gritting his teeth, he walked awkwardly to the door and braced himself against the jam.

His left leg pinched and seized each time he pulled it forward, causing him to drag it lamely. His right leg worked well enough. The pain was tolerable. He addressed the empty hallway. "I think I'll check myself out, without the aid of a wheelchair."

With a final deep breath, he limped down the hall and didn't look back.

A Stranger in The Gym

THE GYM'S FIRST SOUNDS of life creaked and echoed from upstairs.

Cosmo had been up for an hour, hunched over the slop bucket and leaning on the mop. He had mopped the main level first. As he finished the basement of the weight training facility aptly named "The Gym," he envisioned the owner and head coach, Bhupinder Dhawan, re-straightening equipment Cosmo had already aligned.

Bhupinder's footsteps echoed on the cement steps leading to the basement. The kindly owner flipped the lights on. "Why do you insist on working in the dark?"

"Why waste electricity?" Cosmo straightened with difficulty. With the lights on, he scanned the room to ensure he'd done a quality job. He had.

"I think you like the darkness. It's not healthy." Bhupinder tapped the side of his own head. "Get your mind healthy, and your body will follow."

Cosmo sighed while depositing the mop and bucket back in their place. "My body is broken. I broke it."

"Nonsense. You think you're the only young man who has made mistakes? You think I haven't done bad things?" Bhupinder shook his head. "Perhaps if I live to be a shriveled old man, I will have done more good. Vishnu knows."

Cosmo stared at the man who'd given him a job and a place to sleep. Bhupinder had been welcoming and friendly when no one else had. He had trusted Cosmo. Still, Cosmo had no response. "I'm ready to carry a load of towels to the washers. Are there more upstairs?"

"Here, eat something."

Cosmo lowered his gaze.

"Take it, Cosmo. My wife always cooks too much." Bhupinder placed a bowl covered with a towel on a nearby bench. "Look at me." He shook his belly with both hands. "My athletes will stop paying attention, I've grown so fat."

"I'll work for it."

"I know you will. You always do." Bhupinder gripped Cosmo's shoulder. "I'm doing you no favors, young man. Truthfully, I'm taking advantage of you. No one else has taken such good care of my gym for so little in return." With a smile he turned to go. "Oh, there are more towels upstairs. If you would have turned on the lights, you would have seen them."

"Sorry, Coach—"

"Nonsense. Eat your breakfast. Too many smelly gym rags on an empty stomach isn't healthy for anyone. You can bundle the towels after the morning rush." Bhupinder disappeared up the stairs.

Cosmo headed straight for the bowl of curry. He had smelled it before Bhupinder had flipped on the basement lights. He lifted the towel. Instantly the odors carried him away. He closed his eyes and allowed himself to leave the gym basement. Palm trees rooted on a sandy beach temporarily replaced weights and mirrors and smelly rags.

Bhupinder called the dish mutton vindaloo, based on cuisine from Southern India. Cosmo was developing a taste for it. He sat and held the bowl beneath his chin. In this case, the steamed rice steeped in a bowl of mutton curry.

As he gobbled down the dish and licked the bowl clean, Cosmo wondered if Bhupinder had come from Southern India or perhaps married from there. In his five months of living and working in the gym, Cosmo had never asked the jovial owner any personal questions.

Securing the empty bowl in his locker, Cosmo limped upstairs to finish the rest of his duties before the first regulars turned up for their morning workout. On the way, he wondered if Bhupinder was right.

Perhaps languishing in the dark and thinking of nobody but himself wasn't healthy. Here he was, six months after the doctor had given him six months until paralysis, and Cosmo was still waiting for it to happen.

No money. No school. No certificate. No martial arts. No fighting. No life.

Bhupinder had spotted the heart of the matter. Cosmo's mind was broken worse than his body. Instead of counting the days until he could no longer walk, he should be thanking God for every opportunity. Whatever the future might bring, Cosmo had to rely on God's plan for his present.

Cosmo bundled the towels in a corner and hurried downstairs. A small window of time remained before paying customers would need the equipment. Cosmo stood in front of a punching bag for a long minute and wrestled his inertia.

He glanced in the mirror covering the wall. He'd lost weight. His stomach gurgled and he suddenly saw the boy clutching a package of hawai mangan wrapped in used notebook paper. He tasted the spicy beans, felt the hollow ache. He remembered the scream of his mother when he offered her a handful of snakes.

Cosmo was not that boy anymore. But he remained bound by the promises he'd sworn during those years—to take what was his, to never show weakness. Yet, for all his striving, for all his hard work, he hadn't even a handful of snakes.

He hadn't helped his people. He hadn't helped himself. If God had given him a second chance, Cosmo had done nothing with it. For all he knew, time could be running out. *Healthy mind, healthy body.* Cosmo lingered on Bhupinder's favorite mantra.

Grimacing, he stretched his back and rolled his head from side to side. Sounds of life echoed from upstairs. Now or never. He hadn't struck a bag or tried a kick in six months. Not since the morning he coughed up blood in a gym only kilometers away.

After a deep breath, Cosmo focused on the bag and exhaled through his nose. Blocking out everything else, he spun, raised his leg head-high, and struck the bag.

With a thud, his heel dented the heavy canvas. The chain holding up the bag jerked. Cosmo held his stance, his leg frozen in the air a centimeter from the surface it had just struck. His balance remained perfect. A thrill coursed through him, overriding the ache in his back.

The discipline remained in his blood. Broken body or not, maybe Cosmo could still do something with it—something selfless. Rather than telling God what that something was, he would finally listen. He would follow God's lead—wherever it took him.

Getting a Job

"YOUR EXPERIENCE MORE THAN qualifies you for the job. I'm especially impressed with the hours you logged as a student instructor at Khalsa College." The athletic director of St. Stephens College pushed back his chair and stood.

Cosmo followed his lead.

"Now why don't we head out to the gym so you can show me some of what you would be teaching the students."

Cosmo bowed. "I thank you for the opportunity." He opened the director's door politely. When they reached the gym, Cosmo headed for an empty mat. He disguised his limp by bouncing on his toes. Simultaneously, he stretched his tight back and prayed he'd make it through the next several minutes without looking a fool or paralyzing himself.

After a bow, he started with a mid-level form and advanced quickly. He didn't want to draw out his demonstration any longer than necessary. As he focused on the forms, he forgot about his injury, and his years of training took over.

Barely touching down, he brushed over the surface of the mat like a monkey swinging through the jungle canopy. He cracked the air with crisp movements. After five minutes, he stopped without having broken a sweat, his breathing still steady.

While the director nodded in approval at the demonstration, Cosmo felt nothing less than shock. He had merely hoped not to fall down or lose feeling in his legs. Instead, he discovered an energy he'd forgotten.

"Very nice, Mr. Zimik. I believe I've seen enough. Thank you for your application. I have a few more applicants before making the final decision."

Cosmo bowed. "Of course."

"I can tell you now, you are among the top candidates. You'll hear one way or the other by the end of next week." The director extended his hand, and the two men shook while bowing. "Oh, and feel free to have a look around if you're interested in seeing more of the facilities. I apologize for not being able to show you myself."

"No need. I would not expect a tour before getting the job." Cosmo smiled.

"Right. We'll see, Mr. Zimik." The director returned the smile. "Good day."

"Blessings." Cosmo called after him. After the director strode out of sight, Cosmo ran his hand through his hair and laughed. St. Stephens was the most reputable college in Delhi. A coaching job here would open up real opportunity. And Cosmo liked the way teaching satisfied him.

"Excuse me."

Cosmo turned to see a burly Indian, dressed like a government official, grinning ridiculously at him. "Yes?"

"I hope you don't mind me saying, but that display of Burmese Thaing was the best I've ever seen."

Cosmo narrowed his eyes. The man's dress and manner screamed government agent. And a government agent who knew Thaing was one to be avoided. "Thank you." Cosmo bowed slightly and started to walk away.

"I'm not just saying that to be nice. As much as I've tried, I have a hard time being phony that way."

Cosmo gave the man a second look. Broad shouldered and muscular, the man stood several inches taller than Cosmo and had forty kilos on him easily. A deep scar started behind his ear and disappeared beneath his collar. Everything except for his ridiculous grin put Cosmo on edge.

"Sorry, let me introduce myself." The man extended his hand. "The name's Mark."

Cosmo shook Mark's hand, the grip solid but not threatening. Cosmo didn't offer his own name. Old habits died hard, and he had no reason to trust this stranger named Mark.

Despite Cosmo's aloofness, Mark never stopped grinning. "I work for an organization called Athletes in Action. You heard of them?"

Relaxing a little, Cosmo shook his head. Maybe the guy wasn't government. Either way, Cosmo didn't want to waste more time figuring out what he wanted.

Mark continued. "No? Well, I'm hoping to do something about that. AIA is a Christian ministry focused on sharing the Good News of Jesus Christ through sport."

Cosmo nodded. Now the situation made sense. Mark was a missionary bashfully trying to create a convert.

"You're familiar with the Christian Gospel?"

"I and my family are Christian, yes." Cosmo said.

Mark nodded. "I thought as much. I'm no expert, mind you, but I'm starting to develop an eye for the different ethnic groups in Delhi. Don't be offended if I'm wrong, but you strike me as northeast Indian?" He ended the statement as a question.

Cosmo granted Mark an impressed nod. Now he was confused again. If the missionary suspected Cosmo to be a Christian, why were they talking? He started for the door. "I thank you again for the compliment."

Keeping up with Cosmo, Mark got to the point. "What I wanted to ask you was whether or not you're still looking for a job."

"No thank you." Cosmo rolled his eyes. A job as a Christian missionary working for an Indian? The thought was laughable.

The foreign ministry groups he'd been involved with at Khalsa College had never shown the first sign of competence. They never spoke any language other than English. They spent more time eating and drinking tea than talking about God. And they didn't seem to care the slightest bit for the plight of India's countless poor.

"It would be a paid position." Mark followed him to the gym

exit. "Sort of."

"Not interested."

"At least let me share the vision. If you came here to apply for a coaching position, you must love teaching and martial arts."

Outside the building, Cosmo turned on the man. "Yes, but that doesn't mean—"

"I'll buy you lunch." Mark never stopped smiling.

Cosmo caved. He had less than 200 rupees to his name and hadn't eaten since yesterday. "I pick the place."

"Absolutely."

Cosmo took a moment to think. He looked up and down the busy street. If this man was buying, he wanted to take full advantage. He knew just the place. He hadn't eaten there since his prizefight days. For a liberal-spending missionary, the prices wouldn't raise an eye. "You have money for a rickshaw?"

Mark nodded. "I'll pay the whole way. All you have to do is hear me out and be willing to pray about my offer."

"Deal." Cosmo jogged to the curb and motioned for an auto rickshaw.

"Oh, and tell me your name." Mark kept pace beside him.

"Cosmo Zimik."

"Nice to meet you, Cosmo."

Two rival autowallahs, who'd been waiting outside the college, raced for the potential passengers. Cosmo had no doubt they'd spotted Mark's posh attire. The winner scraped into the curb in front of them.

Cosmo scooted across, offering the curbside seat to Mark. "On the way to the restaurant you can tell me your experience with martial arts. I'm not saying I'm not good." Cosmo grinned. "But I'm curious what you have to compare me to."

Herding Goats

THE RATTLING BUS TRANSITIONED from sprawling farmland to forested foothills soon after nightfall. A few hours later the driver stopped for fuel and a short nap. After a trip to the toilets, the students returned to the bus. Some fell asleep while others chattered in low voices near the back.

In the front seat, just behind the doors, Cosmo remained vigilant until the driver awoke and resumed their trip northward toward the Himalayas. Invisible in the darkness, Cosmo knew the mountains watched their approach.

Mark yawned and shifted in the seat next to him.

Cosmo couldn't believe the course of events over the last nine months, or the impact Mark had orchestrated in his life.

Three months after meeting Mark at St. Stephens, Cosmo had quit his job with Bhupinder Dhawan. A month later, Dhawan had led the Indian team to a gold medal in the World Bench Press Championship. Happy for his ex-employer, Cosmo didn't regret moving on.

Mark helped him pay for an apartment he now shared with other Athletes in Action staff. Mark had also helped Cosmo recognize the difference between intimidating people and interesting them in what he had to say. Mark had taken on the role of teacher and mentor before Cosmo knew he was open to being mentored.

For the last six months, Cosmo had been splitting his time between coaching martial arts at St. Stephens and working for Mark with Athletes in Action. Instead of pining for his old friends and his old way of life, Cosmo focused on learning from Mark's expert instruction in the Christian faith.

The more Cosmo shed his layers of anger and the need to prove himself, the more he found satisfaction in simple tasks. He learned it was one thing to face a Goliath in humility, and quite another to face the mundane with the same humble enthusiasm.

"Thank you." Cosmo spoke softly into the hushed mood on the darkened bus.

"For what?" Mark leaned against the window and yawned.

"For letting me come along."

"You know I'm not into doing people favors. I plan on working you like a dog."

"So you're saying this will be a vacation compared to Delhi?"

Mark scoffed. "Always with the persecution complex. Are all Nagas as personable as you?"

Cosmo scratched his chin. "I'm more amicable than most."

Mark shook with silent laughter and then tried for the hundredth time to shift his bulk into a comfortable position. Soon after that, he fell asleep, leaving only Cosmo and the driver awake. After the driver had insisted he'd be fine, Cosmo let his eyes drift shut.

Cosmo jarred awake and flopped onto Mark as the bus hugged a tight curve. Both men rubbed their bleary eyes. Sunrise hadn't yet come to the shadowed side of the Himalayas, but evidence of the sun spilled across the sky above them. Thin wisps of cloud appeared as pink and orange cotton candy clinging to jagged slopes.

Cosmo checked with the driver. He gave the thumbs up and indicated Cosmo had been asleep for three hours.

"How much further to the first village?" Mark stretched his legs beneath the barrier separating the front bench from the stairs leading on and off the bus.

"Not long, if the road remains clear." The driver swerved around fallen rock in the narrow mountain road. "Maybe three hours."

Mark eyed Cosmo dubiously. They both knew three hours was optimistic at best. They'd been on the bus for twelve hours so far. They wouldn't be needed in the village for another six or seven. No need to panic.

Cosmo loosened his back, stretching from side to side. The students were mostly awake but quiet. They stared out the windows as visibility increased. Some listened to music via small earbuds. Cosmo knew Mark had asked the students to leave such lavish devices at home. He made a mental note of the students who had violated the request.

Officially, Cosmo was on the trip as a worker rather than a full participant. Mark had granted him a seat on the bus in exchange for lugging equipment and water, doing dishes and the like. Cosmo was grateful for the opportunity. He'd heard of the success stories associated with the Jesus Film and how effective the ministry had been in tribal areas like the one he'd grown up in.

Despite the kilometers between here and Manipur, Cosmo felt a kinship to the people he'd seen the previous evening. Bustling away from the busy crossroads with heavy burdens strapped to their shoulders, shepherding goats, stopping to stare at a bus full of wealthy Indians—these people were Cosmo's people.

Cosmo wanted to see how the western-orchestrated Jesus Film project reached his people with the Gospel. He wanted to help, if he could.

"What do you think so far?" Mark nodded toward the scenery, now bathed in indirect sunlight. "How does this compare to Manipur?"

Cosmo exhaled. "I understand why the British labeled my home the Naga Hills. They seemed like mountains when I hiked up and down them as a boy. But nothing compares to this."

"Takes your breath away, doesn't it? This is my fourth trip. I'd be shocked if I ever get used to it." The two men rode in silence for several minutes.

The bus slowed and then stopped.

Cosmo stood to see a small herd of goats blocking their progress. Without anyone saying anything, Cosmo assumed this fell under his duties.

The driver swung open the doors.

Cosmo sprang down the steps and into the crisp air. It was June, but the weather gave no indication of the sort of summers Cosmo was accustomed to. Rubbing chills from his bare arms, he smiled and nodded toward two men reclining against the inner slope of the mountain.

They saw him but made no response.

Cosmo worked his way through the clump of goats. "Blessings and good morning." He bowed toward the men.

They continued to squat and gaze up at him.

"English?"

One man rubbed his nose with the back of his hand.

"Hindi?"

No response.

Finally Cosmo tried a traditional greeting in Urdu that he had learned specifically for this trip.

At this the two men perked up. One of the two stood and proceeded to rattle off a longwinded response in a regional dialect that vaguely resembled Hindi.

Cosmo understood enough to recognize it as friendly. He bowed low. Indicating the bus, he asked if he could assist the men in driving their herd toward their final location.

The men looked at each other, discussed something in length, and finally nodded. They looked pleasantly surprised. As flat and expressionless as they had been when Cosmo first approached, they now became equally animated.

One man squeezed Cosmo's hand. Holding it, he led Cosmo to the outer edge of the road. The oily musk of goat rose from his clothing in wafts. After releasing Cosmo's hand, the man handed him a supple stick.

His partner, having reached the head of the herd, clucked his tongue.

Grinning, the first man tutted lightly while tapping the nearest goat on the back. He called something up to his partner and both men laughed.

Cosmo recognized a reference to Christians. It sounded as if the men were laughing at the fact the missionaries had finally sent someone useful.

Cosmo glanced over his shoulder at the bus. Intermittently, the driver moved forward and parked again as the goats progressed along the narrow road. There was certainly room to drive the goats onto the upper slope and allow the bus to pass, but this method seemed more honoring to the men. And they were certainly getting a kick out of it.

Cosmo did his best imitation of the sounds the two men were making. The man beside him nodded approvingly. Baring his teeth, he revealed minor corrections until Cosmo had it down perfectly.

The goats jogged along at a steady pace.

As Cosmo watched the animals, he recognized they had been recently shorn. Perhaps they were now being herded to summer pasture. After forty-five minutes, they reached a trail branching off the main road. Familiar with the way, the goats took the exit without direction.

Both of the herders remained behind to say goodbye. After a long salutation, they bowed deeply and offered namaste.

Cosmo responded in kind.

The two men lingered, as if waiting for further response.

During the men's salutation, Cosmo had recognized the name of the village Mark and the students were headed for. Nodding, he repeated the name of the village.

Smiling, the men turned to follow their goats.

After they'd gone, Cosmo returned to the bus.

"What was that all about?" Mark asked.

Cosmo shrugged. "I think they promised to come see the film this afternoon."

"You never cease to amaze me, Mr. Zimik."

"I'm not even sure what I did."

"Maybe that's why God likes to use you." Mark grinned, his yellow teeth visible.

They Came for a Show

COSMO LOWERED THE PROJECTOR from his back and placed it on the rickety wooden platform the students had assembled minutes earlier. The bus had arrived a couple hours later than the driver had estimated, but in plenty of time for Mark to orientate the students and put them to work.

They fell in beside the full-time Jesus Film crew who had arrived in the village the day before. Cosmo did his best to sort out Mark's directions and those of the film crew. He figured this would be the hardest aspect of his job over the next three weeks.

Right after the bus had arrived, everyone had taken a quick lunch and prayed for the day's event. The little Cosmo had eaten wore off quickly, perhaps due to the altitude. Now they had an hour of preparation remaining until the scheduled show time.

Cosmo backed away from the projector and left the crew to do their thing. Mark tapped his shoulder. "Can you circle around with the water again? Everyone will need to drink more than usual because of the altitude."

"Right." Cosmo headed dutifully toward the five-gallon water jug and lugged it around to each of the students. After they'd each drunk at least a tin cup's worth, Cosmo did the same. He had noticed his head beginning to pound due to the thin air. He hadn't asked how high the village was, but he approximated it at 3,000 meters.

Finished with the water, Cosmo fiddled idly as villagers began to gather. The women wore long saris consisting of bright reds, blues and greens. The older women wore head coverings without masking the red dot in the center of their foreheads.

Mark drew Cosmo aside. "I don't want to make too big of a deal out of it, but the crew tells me they've received frequent threats these past two weeks. It appears not everyone in the area likes the idea of Christians mucking about. Anyway, just keep an eye out."

"One eye or two?" Cosmo scanned the gathering audience.

Mark seemed hesitant to say more. "There's only been one violent altercation, but a few members of the crew were bruised and battered. Anyway, a good place for you would be helping some of the students expand the seating. We've got some crates and things for the older viewers."

Cosmo nodded. Along with a few of the students, he organized the makeshift seating around a rock outcropping the film crew had selected for the showing. If arranged properly, Cosmo thought the area would comfortably seat a hundred people. He didn't know how many were expected.

As he worked on the seating, he noticed a clump of the film crew huddled around the projector. Their agitation level indicated something had gone wrong. Cosmo tasked himself with the job of welcoming and watching villagers. Using the same Urdu greeting he'd given the herders, he became a popular spectacle.

By the time the seating area filled to comfortable capacity, Cosmo grew certain many of the viewers were arriving from outside the host village. He also realized their numbers were going to far exceed what the area could comfortably seat.

With nothing to distract the growing crowd, they focused on the increasing panic of the film crew.

Cosmo broke away from a quizzical clump of locals and asked a student the time. The showing was a half hour late, and people were still arriving. A disturbance arose near the back of the waiting audience, and Cosmo heard several surprised voices.

The crowd separated, stranding a single individual in the open—a large, dark-skinned man, easily a head above the rest. "I came twenty kilometers for a show." The man growled in Hindi. "I'm going to see a show, one way or the other." He drew a machete and thrust it into the air above him.

Cosmo had instinctively advanced toward the man even before seeing the weapon. As the crowd retreated, Cosmo forded through them. He couldn't see the man clearly, but he could hear a string of angry curses.

Some of the filthy language was in Hindi, some in languages or dialects Cosmo didn't recognize. He understood enough. By the time Cosmo reached him, the man had begun growling unintelligibly with a voice so bestial it no longer sounded human at all.

Cosmo motioned for the crowd to stay behind him. As they retreated, Cosmo's presence drew the attention of the angry man.

"I've come for a show. Are you going to give it to me?"

Cosmo responded in Hindi. "We ask your patience as we finish preparations."

"You're late! You're trying to cheat us! Cheating and lies! That's what this is all about!" He pointed toward the film crew with his machete then reverted to cursing.

Cosmo looked to the film crew.

In a panic, they shook their heads. Mark shrugged. With a subtle kill gesture, he indicated the machine had died.

Muttering spread across the crowd. Cosmo wondered how many of them would be just as content to see a fight as a film on the life and death of Jesus. The angry man began to bellow, and Cosmo shifted his full attention toward him.

"I've come for a show one way or the other!" He stepped closer to Cosmo.

"A show then! I'll give you a show!" Cosmo held up a hand, asking the man for another minute. "I'll need a few things first." He hoped enough of the crowd followed his meaning to delay a violent outbreak. He only needed a minute.

"Mark." Cosmo gathered his mentor along with a clump of startled students. "Can you find me some bricks? Maybe some fruit? Oranges, melons, anything I can cut in half."

"Cut in half?"

"A martial arts demonstration. It'll keep them entertained."

Mark nodded. "Sure. Good idea. I'll have the students pull apart the platform for the boards."

"That'll be a good start."

In no time, Cosmo had cleared a flat area directly in front of the angry man and stacked several boards across two upright bricks. Using little rocks placed at either end, he left a finger-width's gap of air between each board.

Satisfied with the makeshift arrangements, Cosmo addressed the curious audience while keeping an eye on the angry man at all times. Cosmo knew the villagers weren't strangers to martial arts, but few masters or schools existed in remote areas. Most likely, they had never seen a formal demonstration of his skill level. At least he hoped.

With a final bit of showmanship and exaggerated focus on his breathing, Cosmo produced a ear-splitting kiai while driving the heel of his fist through the stack of well-aged boards. They splintered unevenly. Shards flew as he continued the punch all the way to the ground and held a pose on a single bent knee.

Before the boards settled to the ground, the crowd broke into applause. Cosmo bowed while observing the angry man. He wasn't clapping, but his eyes were wide open in surprise.

Sensing people behind him, Cosmo turned to find the two herders—one laden with bricks and the other fruit. Grinning, they deposited their loads at his feet and disappeared into the audience.

Cosmo now had enough supplies for a good half hour demonstration.

Kung Fu for Jesus

TOSSING A WATERMELON IN the air, Cosmo sliced it cleanly in half with the blade of his hand and caught the two pieces before they could hit the ground. The villagers laughed and cheered. Even the man with the machete stood relaxed and smiling.

"For my next demonstration, I'll need a volunteer." Cosmo prodded the audience, hoping they understood his Hindi.

"Me!" The man with the machete jumped. "Volunteer. Me!"

Cosmo nodded. The catalyst for his impromptu show seemed an appropriate choice. This called for further improvisation. "Can I borrow your machete?" Cosmo asked.

The man's eyes grew big, then narrowed to slits.

Cosmo stooped to pick up his last remaining apple. He addressed the man again. "All you have to do is stand very still with this on your head." Cosmo indicated his intention to the rest of the audience by placing the apple on his own head.

The crowd gasped and murmured.

The big man flipped the machete in his hand and offered the handle to Cosmo.

Cosmo stretched to place the apple on the man's head before accepting the weapon. A foot taller than Cosmo, the man's height would increase the difficulty of the stunt, along with the thrill.

Cosmo strode into the center of the clearing and pushed aside the larger fragments of fruit with his bare foot. Content with the space, he progressed through some advanced sword forms of Thang Ta.

Lunging and spinning, Cosmo flashed the weapon in the high-altitude sun of a crystal clear afternoon in the Himalayas. He slapped the flat edge of the weapon against his palm and his thigh. In a graceful frenzy, he fought off a dozen invisible attackers.

A blanket of impressed silence fell over the villagers. This was the sort of martial arts they could relate to—a skill every man in the village desired. Half a dozen men trained in this art could defend an entire village.

Short of breath, Cosmo realized he had better finish his final demonstration before he grew too dizzy to perform it safely. Landing on both feet directly in front of the big man, Cosmo barked a single word command in Hindi. "Steady!"

The man transformed into a human statue.

Defying gravity, Cosmo leapt into a windmill kick three feet above the ground. Spinning 360 degrees, he flared all four of his limbs and slashed the machete centimeters over the man's head before landing chest to chest.

A hand's breadth remained between the two men.

Shock filled the big man's eyes.

Cosmo calmly removed the apple from his head. Stepping back, he proffered the handle of the man's machete.

The man took it without blinking.

The audience didn't breathe.

Finally, Cosmo held up the apple in both hands and let it fall into two pieces—sliced cleanly in half.

The villagers thundered with approval. They cheered and laughed and clapped. A show indeed!

Cosmo bowed. As he straightened, lightning shot up his spine. The familiar jolt both terrified him and humbled him.

The nerve damage reminded him that every day he lived with nearly full mobility was a gift. He had unwrapped that gift without gratitude for most of his life. Now he knew better, and he knew what he had to do next.

Parting the crowd, Cosmo leapt onto the remains of the rickety platform built for the projector. He gestured for a microphone.

The members of the film crew stared at each other until Mark prodded one of them. Jumping into action, he scrounged up a microphone, hastily plugged it into the small PA system, and handed it to Cosmo.

In eloquent and clear Hindi, Cosmo reached inside himself and drew out the most intimate aspects of his story. He shared his back and forth dance with God, including the low points he'd never dared reveal to a living soul.

With grateful heart, he poured out the good, the bad and the ugly. He concluded that only by the grace of God could he still walk. Only by the grace of God was he alive despite the countless efforts of others to take the life God had given him.

Cosmo lowered the mic and exhaled a breath of complete and total fulfillment. As enjoyable as campus ministry had been, this was infinitely more so. Before Cosmo's peace could settle, the villagers clambered for more.

They begged to know more about the God of which he spoke.

Cosmo froze, uncertain of what came next. He'd shared everything he had inside him. What more was there?

As if responding to his inward question, Mark appeared at Cosmo's side. The platform groaned under their collective weight. Mark tugged the microphone from Cosmo's grip. "Good job, Mr. Zimik." He nudged Cosmo from the platform.

Cosmo jumped down. Attentively, he listened as his mentor explained the broader truth and finer points of the Gospel message that continued to be better and better news in Cosmo's own life.

An hour later, nearly the entire village, including the man wielding the machete, had committed to the same journey Cosmo had undertaken years earlier. It had taken physical torture to put Cosmo on the path.

He hoped the villagers had not endured as much to arrive at the same place.

Like a peal of thunder in his brain, purpose reverberated within him. Perhaps this was the reason God had given him a second chance. Perhaps Cosmo's years in Delhi had been bumping him clumsily toward this. The nights in the hospital had been a reminder of his second chance.

He could use the very fighting that resulted in his broken body to honor the God of second chances.

Teaching in the Temple

SHAMIL WROTE THE WORDS on the blackboard as Cosmo recited a short passage from the Gospel According to John. At Cosmo's insistence, the partners had agreed to use Biblical texts in their English lessons to the Dalits.

Cosmo tripped over the enshrouded Kali statue as he paced. It had been Shamil's idea to repair the derelict Hindu temple for their classroom. The temple had been abandoned for many years, but the ceiling and walls remained intact. Centrally located, accessible and spacious, the temple worked well—except for the one annoyance.

The glaring image of Kali with her tongue stuck out and numerous arms flailing had been a distraction from the start. For Cosmo at least. The Dalits barely noticed the eight-armed goddess of destruction. Cosmo thought it ugly at best. Within days, he'd covered it with a sheet. Since then he had bumped into the thing no less than once a week.

Putting the statue out of his thoughts, Cosmo checked on the work of the two youngest students in his and Shamil's makeshift English institute for Dalits. Ages five and six, Sanjay and Rajiv were brothers. Their parents attended the classes as well. As usual, the boys learned at a quicker pace than their parents.

"Very good." Cosmo waited for the boys' parents to focus on him as well. He spoke to Sanjay, the eldest son. "Now, can you show me the verb?"

Sanjay identified it correctly without hesitation.

"And the subject?"

Again, Sanjay nailed it.

"Rajiv," Cosmo turned to the younger son, "I saved the hardest for you—the predicate."

Rajiv underlined the appropriate part of the sentence.

Cosmo smiled. "The two of you will be helping your parents speak fluent English before you know it."

"Thank you, teacher." The boys bowed their heads.

Cosmo glanced at their parents who also nodded their thanks.

Everyone who attended the classes contributed their full effort and gratitude. As far as Cosmo knew, no one had ever offered the Dalits an opportunity like this—an opportunity to be on the same footing as everyone else.

Cosmo dedicated most of his time to helping Mark minister to wealthy Indian students on the various campuses around Delhi. He also formed a football team and a martial arts club for the purposes of sharing the Gospel. Sometimes the teams traveled outside the city to perform demonstrations like the impromptu one in the Himalayas over a year earlier.

During those experiences, and experience like this—teaching English to Dalits—Cosmo found fulfillment. While campus ministry was less fulfilling, Cosmo didn't find it difficult. Quite the opposite. Mark and his supervisors seemed to think Cosmo the most effective among their staff.

He tried to explain to the leaders, his effectiveness was simply due to boldness. Rather than pampering the elite students, he oftentimes reviled them. He challenged them and never tolerated their pathetic excuses.

As Cosmo strode through the middle of the English class, he clanked his hip against the statue of Kali and nearly swore out loud. In a huff, he yanked the statue off its pedestal and lugged it into the corner of the room.

When he had finished, he realized most of the students were watching him wide-eyed. Quickly they lowered their heads or looked away.

Shamil waited a moment before drawing Cosmo aside. "What are you doing?"

"I can't stand that stupid thing being in the way all the time."

"You realize most of our students are Hindu, right?"

"What's the big deal. This place isn't a temple anymore. It's a classroom."

Shamil shook his head. "I let you cover it with a sheet at the risk of offending people. Now this?"

Cosmo stared at his partner without expression.

"You just put the goddess of destruction on her back in the corner. You don't find that the least bit blasphemous?"

Cosmo shrugged. "Why should I? I'm not Hindu."

Shamil stammered, unable to come up with a response. "Fine. If there's no objections from the students, we'll leave her there."

"No one's going to object."

"Only because they're scared of you." Shamil fired back, raising his voice a bit too loudly. He regained his composure and continued. "One of these days, you're going to run into some people who aren't afraid of you."

Cosmo nodded, a dumb grin on his face. "It does happen from time to time."

"Just be glad you've got enough beneficial qualities to make up for your annoying ones."

"Why Shamil," Cosmo feigned shock, "that might be the first time anyone has ever admitted that."

Shamil rolled his eyes. "Don't let it go to your head. Just get back to teaching."

"Will do." Cosmo saluted before strutting to the middle of the room, where a nice big opening gave him plenty of room to pace without concern of goddess related pokings.

Battlefield, Part Two

COSMO LOOKED UP AFTER passing the football to one of his teammates. A glint of sunlight on a slender metal object caught his eye. That was when he realized the group of men striding across the field were armed with weapons. A second later, he deduced the Athletes in Action traveling football ministry was not up for the fight.

To make matters worse, they were in the middle of a pickup game with local youth. Some of the kids would be stupid enough to want to fight without the abilities to back it up.

Briefly, Cosmo wondered if he should tell the others to run. Then he noticed the game had stopped. Most of the others had seen the approaching gang. Nervously, they looked to Cosmo for guidance.

If they ran now, it might encourage their attackers to pursue. Plus, it would bode poorly for their future rights to use the field. While Cosmo didn't want to put the kids at risk, he wanted to teach them to stand up for themselves in an intelligent manner. Hopefully, this would play out as a positive teaching moment and not a painful lesson.

When the mob drew closer, Cosmo identified their ringleader—a Hindu militant named Raju. Quickly, he formulated a plan.

This wasn't a team or club wanting to fight for use of the field. At the very least they had come to humiliate Cosmo personally, or to put a stop to the AIA ministry. Raju had long been offended by Cosmo's ethnicity and religious beliefs.

In addition to Raju's religious affiliation, he liked to think of himself as a pure warrior. He and Cosmo had faced off twice before: once in an official martial arts tournament and once in a similar manner to this. Cosmo had won the tournament but lost in a scrape between Raju's militants and Cosmo's martial arts class.

This time, not only had Raju brought a few dozen friends, but they were armed. Some carried knives. Some carried less elegant weapons such as pipes and bats.

As the gang came within earshot, Cosmo spoke first. "Sorry, but you're late."

"Late for what?" Raju's eyelids drooped, an almost bored look on his pockmarked face.

"Practice just ended."

"On the contrary, instruction is about to begin." Raju replied.

The expressions of the thirty plus men backing him up spoke of anger and religious zeal—things Cosmo understood personally. Their looks told him the militants had come here to fight, not to intimidate. This fact reduced Cosmo's options further. He sensed his teammates gathering closer behind him.

"It takes thirty armed men for you to teach me this lesson?" Cosmo chose to target Raju's warrior pride—something he knew the man carried close to the surface.

Raju ground his teeth. His lids drooped even further until Cosmo could barely see his eyes. "Merely a precaution."

"Oh?" Cosmo raised his brows. He glanced toward his teammates and the ragamuffins they had been attempting to get to know. "Against what? If you're worried about guardian angels, you should have brought more men."

Cosmo made an exaggerated effort at counting the militants before returning his attention to Raju. He scratched the back of his head. "Maybe my math isn't so good, but three dozen vs. some kids and football players—"

"Enough talk." Raju motioned for his men to advance.

Cosmo dropped his weight while raising his voice. "So you're afraid to teach me a lesson by yourself?"

"Shut your filthy mouth, *bahadur*, before I shut it for you."

Cosmo growled. "A fair fight, that's all I'm asking for."

"Fair. Ha." Raju spit.

"Fight club rules." Cosmo continued. "You win, I never come here again."

"You still don't get it."

"Enlighten me."

Raju blinked for a full second. "You can't possibly think you can desecrate a Hindu temple and get away with it. Or are you just that arrogant?"

"What are you talking about? Desecrate a—" It took a moment, but Cosmo finally realized what Raju's friendly visit was all about. He laughed. "This is about taking down that Kali statue?"

"You admit it?" Raju hadn't expected this.

"Sure. The stupid thing kept poking me. And that annoying red tongue—"

"Take 'em."

"Wait!" Cosmo flailed his arms, stopping the melee in the nick of time. "Fine. You win and I'll put back the statue. I'll return the whole temple to the faithful Hindus who abandoned it." The deal was no skin off Cosmo's teeth. If he lost, he suspected he'd be dead by the time Raju and his so-called precautionary army were done with him.

"If I win," Cosmo paused. He hadn't been sure where his thoughts were leading until now. As if struck by a bolt of lightning, his body tingled as he spoke the words. "If I win, you and all your men listen to everything I have to say for five minutes."

Raju glanced at the men on either side of him. They shared quizzical looks. "I win, you replace the statue and never show your face around here again?"

Cosmo nodded. "Agreed."

The two opponents thrust their followers backward to clear a ring in the grass. The Hindu militants stumbled to get out of each other's way while Cosmo and Raju circled each other three times.

Raju was good. Both he and Cosmo were trained in kung fu as well as multiple other martial arts. And if Cosmo slipped, Raju's overwhelming numbers would guarantee Cosmo didn't get back up.

He blinked his eyes shut and shot up an arrow prayer.

Raju used the opportunity to launch his attack. Cosmo blocked with both hands to the right. Slamming his back into Raju's chest, Cosmo dropped his weight and used Raju's momentum to throw him.

Raju landed expertly and rolled onto his feet—suffering nothing more than grass stains. Both men closed the distance. Raju revealed an inclination to go low, and Cosmo responded to it.

A split second later, Raju attempted to hyperextend Cosmo's knee. Cosmo had already left the ground with a flying knee kick. Their bodies collided, Cosmo's knee to Raju's shoulder.

As Raju attempted to spin away from the impact, Cosmo grappled for control over his opponent's neck and head. The pair spun 180 degrees in midair before slamming down to earth.

Raju hit hard on his back.

Cosmo aimed a choke at his opponent's throat.

Raju extended his legs and threw Cosmo off.

Aware of the able bodies forming a ring around him, Cosmo scrambled quickly to his feet.

Raju was slower to rise.

Cosmo covered the space between himself and his fallen opponent in a single stride and delivered a vicious kick to Raju's side.

Raju partially blocked while rolling from his back to his stomach. He tried to push upward.

Cosmo kicked him again, this time landing a full blow to Raju's ribs. The kick lifted his opponent several centimeters off the ground and ended the fight. Cosmo knew he had at least cracked a rib, if not broken one.

Cosmo slowed his breathing while maintaining his vigilance. Visually, he stood down each of the militants. If Cosmo remained in control of the situation, Raju's followers might honor the agreement—depending on Raju's lead.

Raju grunted from where he lay on the ground.

Cosmo stooped to help his opponent onto hands and knees. He hoped he hadn't done any lasting damage to the man. "Can you breathe?"

Raju wheezed and coughed into his hand. When he pulled it away, there wasn't any blood.

Cosmo relaxed. "You're lungs are intact. You'll be good as new in a couple months."

"You're really annoying, you know that?" Raju shoved him.

"So I've been told." Cosmo stood, keeping his eyes on the rest of the militants.

Raju growled. "Just get it over with."

Cosmo shook his head. "It's over already."

"Five minutes." Gripping his side, Raju rose to his knees. "Not a second more."

During the fight, Cosmo had forgotten his end of the agreement. When Raju mentioned it, the lightning returned. Cosmo jolted to life, his fight high returning. Instead of a physical fluidity, the energy coursed through his thoughts. It manifested in the form of his father's teaching on King David and personal humility. All at once, Cosmo's life lessons flooded his mind.

He sat and let the words course from his lips as naturally as Thaing coursed through his body. He taught them as if the wisdom were second nature to himself, though he barely understood the concepts. In brief, he shared his story, much like he had in the Himalayas. This time, he adapted the words for men who knew nothing but violence.

By the end of five minutes, every Hindu militant, as well as Cosmo's teammates together with the street kids, had surrendered their rapt attention. Eagerly, they waited for Cosmo to continue. But at the end of the allotted time, the words dried up.

Cosmo breathed deeply. His mind became a vacuous pit. There was nothing left to do but stand and leave. Springing to his feet, he bowed low. He and his teammates ushered the kids off the field.

"Maybe it's time to go for tea." Cosmo couldn't believe he suggested it, but under the circumstances, it made sense to default to Mark's style of teaching. Maybe at the cafe one of his teammates would come up with what to say next.

Kumar Returns

COSMO FINISHED THE CONVERSATIONAL instructions in English and ensured the class successfully partnered off. As soon as everyone engaged in the exercise, Cosmo turned to erase a section of the chalkboard and write the new vocabulary words. When he did, he spotted a newcomer standing in the door—Kumar.

Cosmo returned the eraser to the sill and strode calmly to the temple entrance. Kumar had come alone and without his ridiculous knee-high socks. In a low tone, Cosmo addressed the Hindu militant he'd left beaten and bruised on the cricket field two years earlier. "Can I help you?"

Kumar stared past Cosmo into the temple classroom for a long few seconds. He ran his hand over his face and sighed. "I've been paid 1,500 rupees to kill you."

Cosmo tensed. "So little?"

Kumar shrugged. "I suppose if it had been more, we wouldn't be talking."

Cosmo nodded. "What exactly are we talking about?"

"I wanted to see for myself." Kumar nodded toward the classroom. "Raju claimed you were turning Dalits into Christian zealots, that you were defacing Hindu temples."

Cosmo tried to appreciate what he and Shamil were doing from an outside perspective. He understood how charitable work among the Dalits could make people nervous. The Dalits were so numerous, if someone was able to wield them in a personal cause, their power would be great. "You didn't believe him?"

"It didn't sound like the Cosmo Zimik I remembered from the cricket field. An arrogant jerk, sure. Defacing sacred sites, maybe. But the Dalits? That part didn't fit." Kumar shook his head. "No, the Cosmo I knew could have recruited a hundred Naga students and turned them into warriors in a matter of weeks."

"I suppose you're right." Cosmo checked over his shoulder to make sure the class was fine without him. It was. "What do you think now?"

"Is all this for real?" Kumar asked.

"What exactly?"

"You giving your time and energy to them—teaching the Scheduled how to speak English. Playing football with street kids. This." He gestured toward Cosmo.

Without hesitation Cosmo answered. "Yes, more real than anything I've ever done."

"That's what I thought." Kumar turned to go.

"What do you plan on doing next?"

Kumar spoke without turning around. "I'm going to give back the money."

"Do you mind me asking why?" Cosmo called after him.

Kumar stopped in the middle of the sidewalk, forcing people to swerve around him. He turned to look Cosmo in the eyes. "I'm from a Backward Caste myself. I've never met a Hindu willing to serve the Dalits, despite worshiping the same gods. And yet, you worship another." He shook his head. "Someone will kill you yet, Zimik. But it won't be me."

Cosmo couldn't be sure, but he thought he heard the parting words, 'Be careful,' before Kumar disappeared into the flow of pedestrian traffic.

PART 5

Loose Cannons

Parting Ways With AIA

THE KNOCK CAME LIGHTLY on the door. Cosmo had been expecting it. He rose from the couch and let Mark into the apartment.

Mark almost had to duck to enter.

Cosmo flipped on additional lighting. He'd been trying to talk to God for the last half hour, but kept finding himself distracted by the impending conversation.

Mark greeted Cosmo by grabbing his hand and shoulder for a firm shake.

"Anything to drink?" Cosmo offered.

Mark shook his head, then changed his mind. "A Pepsi."

Cosmo fetched his mentor a cola from the small fridge and split it between two glasses without ice. He placed them on the low table and took a seat on the couch next to Mark.

"I've taken the matter to anyone who'd listen." Mark sipped his cola.

"And?"

"I'm afraid there will be no compromise, no negotiation. It's not how the ministry works. We have hundreds of missionaries—thousands. We can't make special rules—"

"But this is not what I'm called to do." Cosmo objected.

Mark sighed. "Calling can be fickle, influenced by mood or fad."

"You think I'm too—"

"It's not about what I think, Cosmo." Mark put a hand on Cosmo's shoulder. "It's about the skills and abilities God has given you. It's about the needs of those we serve."

"Or is it about the skills that serve your superiors' needs?"

Mark closed his eyes and exhaled.

Cosmo continued. "I'm tired of feeling used for the things I can do, or for the places I can open for the rest of you."

"You've been put in a unique position. Are you saying you would like God to reconsider?" Mark asked.

"I'm saying I would like Athletes in Action to reconsider."

"They won't, Cosmo. There are already ministries, hundreds of them, working in the slums and the villages. You know better than anyone, there is next to nothing for students. The ministry will not change its focus for a single staff worker."

"Then just reassign me to the Jesus Film. I can use my skills there."

"Absolutely you could, along with thousands of other high school students." Mark turned toward Cosmo. "The Jesus Film is a well oiled machine. It's set up so any fifteen-year-old can help. Your talents would go to waste. Do you know how many people can do what you've been trained to do on campus? What you've done so easily and so effectively over the past two years overshadows the last several years of my own efforts."

Cosmo shook his head. "It's hollow. My heart's not in it."

Mark took a long drink. "No one will stop you from following your heart. I've come here this evening to tell you, that if you do so, it will not be with Athletes in Action."

Cosmo swallowed. "Or with you."

"My ministry is to student athletes. That hasn't changed."

"Of course." Cosmo stood, unsure of what he had expected.

Mark stood as well. "But neither has my friendship with you. Just because we won't work together, doesn't mean you're not a friend and partner in the faith."

The two stood in silence for several seconds before Mark continued. "And if you don't mind me saying, a spiritual son."

"Thank you," Cosmo said.

"For what?"

"For everything. For approaching me that first time at St. Stephens. For teaching me. For believing in me. For seeing something in me I couldn't see myself."

Mark grinned. "I still see it."

Cosmo raised a brow. He wasn't sure what Mark was getting at.

"Hey, lighten up." Mark headed for the door. "You eaten yet?"

Cosmo shrugged. "Not lately."

Mark rolled his eyes. "Let's get some dinner."

Cosmo hesitated, a sly look on his face.

"Don't worry, it's on me." Mark opened the door. "As usual."

Another Author's Note

KUMAR (A PSEUDONYM) BECAME close friends with Cosmo during and after his years with Athletes in Action. In fact, only months after being paid the equivalent of $18 USD to kill Cosmo in 1995, Kumar abandoned his beliefs in Hinduism to adopt Cosmo's Christian ideology.

During 1996 and 1997, the new friends and missionaries to the poor found themselves repeatedly in trouble for sharing their personal encounters with Jesus the Christ. Along with Kumar, a dozen others who had once regarded Cosmo as an enemy changed sides when they witnessed the radical reorientation in his life. Many of these converts remain friends to this day.

Unfortunately, others have since died. Raju also shifted his allegiance to Christianity only to be cut down by his former Hindu brothers in arms a few years later. His widow was swiftly relocated in order to prevent further contact with Cosmo and his fellow Christians.

There are many other stories from this period (and every period) of Cosmo's life waiting to be told. Some of them remain too sensitive to disguise with pseudonyms and altered locations.

Our efforts to contact people, to gain permission for their inclusion, have met with mixed results. Many of the young people Cosmo impacted during his years of ministry in Delhi have indicated they fear reprisal from government investigative agencies and militants.

Overall, the ministry Cosmo started after his years with Athletes in Action led a much more nuanced existence than I'm able to portray during the following chapters. In short, Cosmo and his comrades took up any opportunity they could find to reach out to their types of people—from distributing the Comic Bible to schools, to filming Coca-Cola commercials, to attending the Olympics as spiritual counselors.

The forces that would eventually lead to Cosmo's transition from this season of his life to the next were numerous. Some are better left outside the scope of this book.

I apologize once again for the necessary censorship. Perhaps future reconciliation, both politically and religiously, will allow the story to be shared in its entirety. Until then, the edited version you have before you must suffice. Please, pardon this final interruption as I return you to the story in the spring of 1996, just after Cosmo's twenty-sixth birthday.

Leaps and Bounds

"WHERE IS THIS PLACE again?" Kumar turned in his seat to talk to Cosmo, who was seated behind him in the seventeen-passenger van.

"Just outside Gurgaon."

"We were outside of Gurgaon a half hour ago."

"Just South of Gurgaon." Cosmo corrected himself.

Kumar nodded. "I know of a perfect place for dinner on the way home."

"Another ministry expense?" Cosmo's cousin, Kachui, joined in the conversation as the van slowed to a crawl in midday traffic. The driver slammed his arm on the outside of the driver-side door. With his head out the window, he chided an autowallah attempting to create an extra lane.

Cosmo waited for the ruckus to die down. "That's why we brought you along, cousin."

"To limit stray spending?" Kachui shot back.

"No, to raise enough money for us to have dinner." Kumar leaned across to punch Kachui in the arm, perhaps a bit harder than necessary.

"Watch it, hit man." Kachui used the insider nickname the group had given Kumar after he joined their ministry. Tongue in cheek, the inner core of the group used the name when no one else was listening. On this instance the driver cocked his head to the side.

Kumar glared at Kachui. "Good thing the going rate on you never got over 200 rupees."

Cosmo snickered. "I feel honored to have reached 1,500."

"There's no hit on me, and we all know it." Kachui said. "I haven't gone around picking fights with everyone who looks at me crooked."

"Those are fighting words." Cosmo over exaggerated his offense.

"Cut it out." Kachui didn't flinch. "Since we're on the issue of money…"

Kumar interrupted. "I thought we were on the issue of dinner."

"We haven't even had lunch yet." Cosmo said.

Kachui threw a sack lunch at his cousin. "Have a sandwich." Kumar started to complain, but Kachui hit him with a second brown bag before he could get a word out. "Maybe with some food in your mouths I'll be able to carry on a one-sided intelligent conversation."

"Whatever you say, boss." Kumar pulled out a grilled paneer sandwich. "What, no meat?" He picked a tomato slice out of the sandwich and gobbled it down.

"I'll have you know, I found those sandwiches in the dumpster behind Bukhara Cafe, hardly touched."

Kumar stopped in the middle of a huge bite.

Cosmo slapped the back of Kumar's head. "You have to learn when my cousin is joking."

Kumar chewed and swallowed. "Whatever."

"Anyway, as I was going to say," Kachui resumed, "the ministry is growing too quickly for the money to keep up."

"We always have money when we need it," Cosmo said.

"You say that as if you have something to do with it." Kachui shook his head. "And besides it's not even true. Usually we decide what we need based on available resources. It's not the same thing."

"It's the same thing to me." Cosmo spoke with his mouth full of grilled paneer.

"What about tomorrow's three demonstrations in the Jahangir Puri district?"

Cosmo shrugged.

"Are you aware we only have enough bricks for one show?" Watching the others eat, Kachui decided to start on a sandwich of his own.

Kumar picked up the conversation. "What about the demolition of the old Azadpur building? There's gotta be some salvageable bricks there."

"Good thinking, hit man." Cosmo wiped his chin. "We'll stop tonight and see what we can find."

"Bottles? Coconuts? Pine boards?" Kachui resumed the interrogation. "We're nearly out of everything. Or do you plan on breaking their spirits for your final act?"

Cosmo nodded. "Okay. Point taken, cousin. This is why I hired you. I'll make a round for donations first thing tomorrow morning. Do you have a list of the building supply places we've hit up?"

Kachui nodded. "What about the football match Friday evening?"

Cosmo sat up straight, putting on his business face. "Do the new guys have shoes?"

"Yes, and shirts. But we'll need to buy refreshments."

"Can you get enough money today to cover it?"

Kachui raised a brow. "Sixteen teams?"

"You think there'll be that many?" Kumar asked.

"Three weeks before the Kenya Open?" Kachui asked rhetorically.

Cosmo scratched his chin. "I could kill a few extra dogs."

"Nothing beats fresh grilled dog." Kumar licked his lips.

Kachui remained unimpressed. "It'll take more than dog to buy the right to share with over a hundred sweaty football players, most of whom will be Muslims."

"It's not like we'll be offering pig." Kumar scrounged on the floor beneath Kachui for another brown bag.

Kachui slapped his hand.

Kumar reared back in preparation to tackle the team treasurer.

Cosmo snatched Kumar by the collar, preventing the fight. "Just see what you can do, cousin. If the Gurgaon churches wish to partner in the future, perhaps they'll be willing to fund the present. We can send them fresh converts. Today will be proof enough of that."

Kumar gave up his struggle to retaliate against Kachui. "You sound pretty sure of yourself, brother. This is our first show in Gurgaon. The Hindus in the area are more vigilant than Delhi. I've taken money for jobs," Kumar hung his head. "Any little thing is worth killing over around here."

"This isn't a little thing. You're proof. I'm proof. We'll give them a show, and we'll show them the truth." Cosmo turned from Kumar to Kachui. "We just need money a day at a time. I don't want to stop scheduling events in the future because we don't have money today. This is God's business. We're here to manage it."

"Fair enough. I'll do what I can." Kachui finished his sandwich.

"And so will we." Cosmo glanced over his shoulder at the other dozen volunteers riding in the back of the van. Some of them had been with him since he first formed his ministry, The Winning Team, three months earlier. A few of them were so fresh, he struggled to remember their names.

Before they arrived for the martial arts demonstration south of Gurgaon, he'd need to go over the basics again: respect the locals, defer when confronted, show strength but restraint in all situations. Above all, remember why they've come—to share how Jesus the Christ has impacted their lives.

When in doubt, watch and learn. Cosmo didn't have time to spend days or even hours on training. Too many people were starving all around him, both physically and spiritually. This was ministry by fire.

That included himself. At times, doubt reared its ugly head. He remembered the jungle ministry of his father. Despite his father's years of faithful service, God had regularly failed to provide food for their table.

But this wasn't the jungle. This was Delhi. Cosmo knew money flowed like rivers beneath the city's dirty surface. He knew where to find it, and he knew the sort of talk it took to procure it, even if Kachui didn't.

God's work would be done, one way or the other.

The Big Event

THEY ARRIVED AT THE large, urban village south of Gurgaon an hour past noon. Weekday, weekend, it didn't matter to Cosmo when they scheduled the demonstrations. His people always showed up—the poor, the jobless, the listless, students, porters on break. Whoever they found, they invited.

The driver parked the van in an alley behind the house of the village chief. This chief lived in a two story house constructed from both cinder block and baked brick. Cosmo blessed Kachui on his mission to raise funds and sent him off in an auto rickshaw to meet with a local pastor named Anil.

In front of the chief's house the team found a small wooden stage, made mostly from pallets, ready for their demonstration. Cosmo scanned the courtyard. Palm trees lined the end nearest the chief's house. Low stone walls ran along either side. The front lay open to the commercial section of the village. A handful of scattered benches and grassy spots would accommodate a few hundred onlookers.

It was as good of a place as any. And he liked the fact the village chief would have no choice but to be aware of their presence. Of course the chief knew a martial arts demonstration had booked the courtyard. He would learn of their Christian status soon enough—he and the elders and the entire village.

Cosmo sent three quarters of the team out to perform impromptu sparring throughout the surrounding area as advertising for the afternoon's event. He stayed back with the remaining few to supervise the set up of their janky PA system and some scaffolding to assist in his breaking of twenty-seven bricks with his head.

The scaffolding was his main concern. Missing several of the hitch and cotter pins, it required some jerry-rigging to ensure it didn't collapse before he could break the bricks and climb down. One good thing about their dwindling funds was that Cosmo couldn't afford enough bricks to stack them very high off the ground. If he fell from today's height, the worst that'd happen would be a few bruises and cuts—as long as the bricks didn't fall on him.

He shrugged off the possibility while fetching a crate of glass bottles from the van. He had been living on borrowed time for the last two years already.

By the designated start-time of the demonstration, a few hundred people had crammed into the courtyard. Children lined the stone walls on both sides. Cosmo liked to think they'd just been dismissed from school. Although he knew many of them probably didn't attend.

Cosmo also caught more than one glimpse of the village chief through his second story window.

Not particularly muggy, the weather was good for an outdoor performance. In general, the audience seemed pleased for the distraction from whatever other mundane matters they had been attending. Cosmo was excited for an opportunity to share his story with Hindus who would have never heard anything like it.

He tested the mic with a finger before addressing the audience in Hindi. "Namaste, and thank you for attending the martial arts demonstration of The Winning Team. My name is Cosmo Zimik."

The audience was unimpressed. Cosmo had grown accustomed to Indian people's responses to his Mongoloid appearance. It made their inevitable shock in the wake of his first stunt that much greater.

He resisted the urge to roll his eyes as he strolled across the creaking stage and stabbed the tips of his fingers through a glass bottle on a chest-high shelf. It shattered. Without setting down the microphone, he caught a second bottle that had been stacked on top of the first one, tossed it nonchalantly over his head and shattered it with a kick.

Wide-eyed and breathless, the audience watched as two assistants whisked away a sheet that had caught the majority of the glass. Only after the sheet had been removed did the cheering begin.

Cosmo held up a hand to silence them. Continuing his prepared words, he spoke of physical power and mental quickness. He asked the audience questions, all while orchestrating a variety of stunts—some performed by himself, some by the rest of his team.

They stacked coconuts on rocks, then crushed them with a punch. They leapt from the stage to sunder boards held by members of the audience. Cosmo broke every last one of the twenty-seven bricks with one fail swoop of his head. They performed choreographed fights with swords and sticks.

Cosmo performed his trademark stunt of slicing an apple in half from the top of someone's head. Now, instead of choosing volunteers from the crowd, he used only trained members of his team.

Cosmo knew much of their martial arts appeared as magic to the Hindu audience. Their religious beliefs accredited such unbelievable acts to different gods of their pantheon. Cosmo used that foundation to explain the source of his life and strength as Jesus the Christ.

He built off the familiarity most Hindus had with Jesus as one god among many. He, and other members of his team, shared their transformative stories. They explained how God was extending the offer to everyone—power, forgiveness, grace.

The demonstration ended with nearly half the audience clambering to know more. They signed follow up cards and handed them in while pocketing the pencils. Using the microphone, Cosmo prayed for the audience members who remained behind.

He and his team mingled afterwards. They did what they could to refer the new converts to the few, small Christian churches in the area. They passed out a couple dozen Bibles to those who seemed most hungry for more. The two dozen copies were their last, and The Winning Team had received those only because they'd been water damaged in a warehouse.

The seeds had been planted. Cosmo would do everything he could to follow up, without slowing his relentless efforts to reach the rest. But there were so many. He had to trust God to run the business.

Church Partners

KACHUI RETURNED AS COSMO oversaw the safe departure of the last dozen young men to leave the courtyard. A small band of Hindu militants had gathered across the street by the end of the demonstration. They kept their distance—their numbers and strength impotent against Cosmo and his trained fighters. Word had no doubt spread of The Winning Team's Christian message.

Cosmo always made sure to speak toward broader topics as well—education, literacy, charity, and the importance of staying off drugs. He wanted government officials to see the charity work and hear his socially empowering message as well as the Gospel. It helped ensure continued invitations in the future.

But the militants—Cosmo knew they heard none of that. He only hoped today's converts wouldn't be hunted down and harassed, or worse. As Cosmo watched to make sure the new converts wouldn't be jumped on their way home, Kachui addressed him from behind.

"I think I found us a new partner."

"Really? How so?"

"Pastor Anil is the real deal. His church is small, but he's mobilizing groups of trained men to start dozens more throughout Gurgaon. He doesn't have much money, but he's interested in our ministry."

"How interested?" Cosmo turned toward his cousin.

"He seems to think of nothing other than God's kingdom. If we show him what we're doing." Kachui glanced around the stage. "Today's conversions were many?"

Cosmo grinned. "Over a hundred."

Kachui whistled through his teeth. He nodded over his shoulder, toward the two-story house of the village chief. The Hindus aren't going to like *that*."

"There's already a get-out-of-town committee across the street."

"On that note," Kachui moved closer to Cosmo and lowered his voice, "Pastor Anil has encountered the same committee. He voiced concern for us. I assured him we could take care of ourselves."

"They've been bullying the church?" Cosmo regarded the huddle of militants on the other side of the four-lane boulevard.

"Mostly vandalism. A few scattered beatings. Lots of intimidation. Anil says he's been warned to be satisfied with one church."

"Or what?"

"The violence will increase."

"How far to his house?" Cosmo asked.

"Not far." Kachui shrugged. "A dozen kilometers. He lives in a gated community out of fear of attack."

"Let's take the van." Cosmo leapt from the stage.

"To make another visit?" Kachui followed.

"Bring the box of conversion cards. I'll give the team the next couple of hours off."

"You think that's a good idea?" Kachui plucked up the box.

Cosmo shrugged. "What kind of trouble could a bunch of Christian ex-thugs and students get into in a mostly Hindu village during the middle of the day?"

Kachui rolled his eyes. "You're the boss."

Cosmo drove while Kachui and Kumar took up the remainder of the first row in the van. Cosmo had given the driver a hundred rupees to overlook the violation that could get him fired if his supervisors found out he let someone else drive the van. The driver took the money happily and waived goodbye as the three drove off.

Cosmo hadn't wanted to bring a stranger, and most likely a Hindu, to the pastor's house. If things were as bad as they sounded, the act could be considered careless at the very least. He zipped across town, following Kachui's directions, and they arrived at the gated community in less than half an hour.

Kachui punched the entry code into a solar powered keypad and the gate opened inward. The fancy gate and solid brick walls revealed a modest community of homes. While they were nicer than even the nicest huts in the village where Cosmo had grown up, they weren't excessive by Delhi standards. The gate was the most expensive piece of modern technology visible.

Cosmo looked to Kumar as the gate shut behind them. "Is the crime in Gurgaon this bad?"

Kumar shrugged. "There are those who feel threatened, and those who make sure of it. Like anywhere I guess."

"Turn left." Kachui pointed. "Anil's is the last house on this drive."

They rolled to a stop in front of the small brick house. Cosmo let Kachui get out first in case Anil was watching from inside. Sure enough, as soon as Kachui jumped out of the van, the pastor opened his front door.

"Brother Kachui, you honor me with another visit so soon." Anil jogged to greet his guests. His energy level seemed excessive.

Kachui greeted him. "When I mentioned all that God is doing through your ministry, my cousin couldn't wait to meet you." Kachui nodded toward Cosmo as he rounded the front of the van. "Pastor Anil, this is my cousin, Cosmo Zimik. And this is our friend and partner, Kumar."

"Ah, the warriors." Anil smiled. He extended a hand and bowed.

"I have been called warrior, among other things." Cosmo shook Anil's hand firmly, as did Kumar.

"The Lord needs all types in his army," Anil said.

"And what type are you, Pastor Anil?" Cosmo buffered the direct question with a friendly glint in his eye.

Anil nodded. "Come, we'll talk inside. I still have some tea warm enough from earlier. Perhaps my wife can conjure up some cakes."

"Well what are we waiting for?" Kumar raised a brow.

"Indeed. Come, I will share with you anything Brother Kachui has not already."

A half hour later, Cosmo had been convinced. Producing a handful of conversion cards from his pocket, he offered the stack to Anil.

"What are these? Or rather who?" Anil scanned the names on the cards.

Kumar slurped his tea after having finished off the last cake made from almond paste and dates.

Cosmo pulled a larger stack of cards from his other pocket. "These are the one hundred plus names of the people from your own village who accepted Jesus as Lord this afternoon at our event."

Anil looked again at the names, scanning them more closely. "I recognize this one. Praise God!" He flipped them energetically. After reaching the end of the first stack, he snatched the one in Cosmo's hand and scurried through each and every card. "Incredible. All these from one demonstration?"

Cosmo laughed. He couldn't resist the pastor's enthusiasm. "This is typical. And some days we perform as many as four times. The harvest—"

"Is indeed plentiful." Anil finished Cosmo's sentence. "I had no idea martial arts could be used in this manner. What of these people?" Anil held up the cards.

"Do you have the resources to follow them up?"

Anil ran his hand over his mouth, a crazy look in his eyes. He calmly organized the cards into a neat pile and placed them on the low table. He picked up his cup of tea and finished it off. After licking his lips, he replied. "I most definitely do. A dozen well-trained men, core group leaders—the ones tasked with starting the new churches. This could be the boost we need to make it happen."

"Then I give them into your care." Cosmo scooted the cards closer to Anil.

Anil bowed. "I'm unspeakably grateful. We have had success with evangelism, but nothing on this scale, and not without—" he hesitated.

"Cost." Cosmo nodded. "I understand. "Kachui mentioned some of the persecution you and your people have faced."

Anil stared at his feet, his hands suddenly trembling. "I, the physical—" he gripped one hand in the other. "This kind of boldness, the kind you know so easily, it is a weakness of mine. One the devil toys with on a regular basis. I know I shouldn't fear—"

"There is always good reason for fear." Cosmo cut him off. "Fear warns us of danger." Cosmo shook his head. "Do not regard me and my ministry more highly than your own, Pastor Anil. For most of my life, I have lived as a violent and angry individual. I have done more shameful deeds than you, I'm sure. My ministry, this is what I must now do for the Lord. As you said yourself, the Lord needs all types in his army. Kumar and I, we are one. You and Kachui are another."

Anil gathered himself.

"Partnered together, we are stronger than apart. Would you agree?"

"Well put, Brother Cosmo, well put. I would very much like to explore partnership with you and The Winning Team."

"Blessings on your ministry, pastor." Cosmo finished his tea. "We will do everything we can to evangelize your village and the surrounding parts of Gurgaon. Then it will be up to you and your men to further their Christian growth."

"Agreed." Anil's vigor and energy returned in full force. He leapt from the couch and scurried to a desk lodged into the corner of the living room and piled high with books. He pulled a drawer completely from the desk and untaped an envelope from the back of it. "It isn't much, but I always save a bit for the unforeseen opportunity. I say this qualifies."

The pastor pulled a clump of wrinkled bills from the envelope—a thousand rupees at least.

Cosmo stood, shaking his head.

Anil pushed it on him. "Think of it as a thank you, for your contribution to my village and my community. I've spent much more on evangelistic efforts with far less results."

Cosmo hesitated. He had hoped Kachui would handle all such

transactions. Although, he wasn't sure why it bothered him. In the past, he'd accepted money in exchange for beating people up. Granted, Cosmo had changed greatly since then. This should be easier on countless levels.

Anil continued. "God is blessing your ministry through me. Take his money and use it wisely."

Cosmo relented. "Thank you, Pastor. Just today my cousin and I discussed funding our three shows tomorrow. As always, God has provided."

"Good then!" Anil clapped his hands. "Blessings, blessings on your ministry. You'll stay for dinner?"

Kumar started to nod in the affirmative, but Cosmo held him back. "Apologies, Pastor Anil, but I left the rest of my team at the village courtyard. We should be getting back to them soon."

Anil widened his eyes. "You performed in the courtyard?"

Kachui jumped in. "We reserved the space two weeks ago. Everything on the up and up."

Anil drummed his fingers on his lips and proceeded to talk more to himself than his guests. "The elders will already know."

"Pastor," Kachui stepped forward, "I hope we have not caused you any additional threat by our performance today."

Anil suddenly flipped his demeanor. "No, no. It's nothing. Don't worry about it. I see how you should be getting back."

Cosmo knew the matter was more than nothing, but he didn't want to embarrass the pastor further. Everyone put on happy faces. They exchanged another round of thanks back and forth before Anil ushered them to the door and waved as they drove off.

Inside the van, Kumar turned to Cosmo with a shrewd look on his face. "Are you thinking what I'm thinking?"

Cosmo nodded. "We've got one more visit to make before leaving town."

Kachui stared across the two of them from his window seat. "Not again. I swear." He threw up his hands. "Every time someone looks at you crooked."

I'll Burn You Down

THE THREE FRIENDS WERE an hour late by the time Cosmo parked the van in the village chief's personal drive. The martial arts team and the van driver were waiting in the courtyard. Cosmo jumped out of the driver's seat and directed the team toward the front door of the chief's house instead of the van.

Kachui remained in the van with his head in his hands, until he eventually decided to join the rest.

Before the team had a chance to question Cosmo's lead, he had knocked on the door. As it opened, everyone fell quiet.

"Purpose?" A big man in a suit with a radio clipped to his belt blocked their entrance.

Cosmo smiled. "My team and I would like to personally thank the chief for allowing us to use his fine courtyard for today's event."

"I'll pass along your thanks." Nearly imperceptibly, the man bowed and moved to close the door.

Cosmo advanced another step, still smiling. "We've prepared a personal demonstration for the chief and elders out of gratitude."

The guard frowned. "Do you have an appointment?"

"Of course." Cosmo lied.

The guard inched a hand toward his radio, testing Cosmo's response. When no one on the martial arts team budged, he held the radio up to his mouth and announced them. After a pause of several seconds the word came back to show the team to the conference room.

The guard replaced the radio on his belt, puffed his chest and stood aside. "The chief will meet you shortly. This way." Then, as an afterthought, "Of course, no weapons are allowed."

"Certainly. The show swords won't be necessary." Cosmo bowed and led the entire fifteen-member team inside. Only the driver remained in the courtyard.

When they reached what the guard had called the conference room, no one on the team bothered asking Cosmo what was up. The ones who'd been around had figured it out on their own. The rest knew enough to keep quiet and pay attention.

Sparsely furnished with a handful of chairs and potted plants, the room felt like a dormitory study lounge. After several minutes of waiting, Cosmo suspected the chief might be using the time to gather the militants from across the street. Gather an army, it wouldn't change things. Everyone has their role in the Kingdom. Living on borrowed time and a pocket full of second chances, this role was Cosmo's.

When the door opened again, the guard from the front door entered first. Following him, a handful of spiffed up militants lined both sides of the entrance and stood with their hands crossed behind their backs. Finally, the chief strode through the door. Eighty plus years had withered his frame, but he stood proudly until Cosmo initiated a bow.

"Honorable chief, thank you for accommodating me and my team."

"You put on quite a show today. A quality performance. I appreciate the emphasis on hard work and charity. Please," the chief motioned toward two chairs turned partially toward each other. "I would offer everyone a seat, but I'm afraid I do not have enough."

"You are most gracious." Cosmo sat after the chief had seated himself. "But my team would be unable to perform properly from a seated position." Cosmo grinned.

"Indeed. My guard mentioned a private performance?"

"More of a request, truthfully."

"Oh?" The chief raised a brow. "Please, you are honored guests."

"Thank you." Cosmo leaned forward, his hands clasped together, his elbows on his knees. "I've recently met with a man of great character and tender heart who lives under your protection."

The chief waited patiently for Cosmo to continue.

"Pastor Anil. Do you know him?"

The chief made an act of searching his thoughts. "His name is familiar. A Christian, is he not?"

"He is." Cosmo nodded. "Of great spiritual vision and power. Sadly, it has come to my attention that Pastor Anil's person, his family and his flock have come under assault from unscrupulous Hindu militants—a renegade lot, I'm sure."

"Unfortunate." The chief pursed his lips.

"While I'm sure you and the elders will do your best to safeguard every member of your village, I am here today to vow my solidarity in that effort."

The chief's eyes grew icy. "Mr. Zimik is it?"

Cosmo nodded.

"While I thank you for your concern, I assure you, me and my people are more than up to the task."

"I've no doubt." Cosmo stood.

The militants along the wall visibly stiffened.

Cosmo's team had gradually sifted into the empty spaces between him and the militants. Now they stood as a single menacing entity.

Cosmo continued in a gentle voice. "Let me be perfectly clear. Whatever your task, me and mine will rise above it. Pastor Anil is a father and a brother, as are anyone who shares kinship in Christ. They are under our protection."

Cosmo scanned the faces of the militants and the guard before returning his gaze to the chief. Creases of anger and fear crinkled around the old man's eyes. Cosmo continued. "We do not practice intimidation, because we do not need to. I do not threaten violence, because I do not want to. But violence against my family will not be overlooked."

Briefly, Cosmo remembered Jesus' sermon to turn the other cheek. His father's teaching on the passage echoed in Cosmo's mind. His interpretation differed slightly.

"Burn my village, I'll burn yours." Cosmo bowed while gesturing to his team. "Thank you for your hospitality." Before the guard or militants had time to receive orders or think twice, Cosmo and his team had exited through the chief's front door.

It was past dinner by the time the van flowed into traffic on the main thoroughfare leading north into Gurgaon. For the majority of the team, the tension had dissolved the moment they exited the chief's house and began loading the van.

Kachui remained tense until the van pulled away. Cosmo still pondered whether he'd done the right thing. He thought again of King David's encounter with Goliath—the story his father had shared with him several years earlier. Routinely, Cosmo's thoughts returned there.

Goliath had insulted the entire nation of Israel. He had spoken against God. David had been the only one unwilling to tolerate the offense. Wasn't this the same thing? Then again, if David's response had indeed been spiritual, rather than martial—Cosmo wasn't sure he could say the same thing about his own actions.

Kumar's rumbling stomach interrupted Cosmo's ramblings. He snapped out of his trance.

Kumar slapped his stomach. "I sure could go for some dinner."

Cosmo nodded. "Give the driver the directions."

Kumar's eyes widened. "You're going to love this place. They make this khubz stuffed with masala. To kill for."

Cosmo frowned. "Fifty rupee limit."

"No problem. The prices are as good as the flavor." Kumar leaned forward to talk into the driver's ear.

Cosmo dug a hand into his pocket and rustled the wad of money there. The bills reminded him of the conversion cards he'd handed over to Anil, along with the hundreds more they would collect tomorrow. The work was happening, and it would continue to happen. That was the important thing.

Grasping Hands

COSMO SLAMMED THE PHONE receiver into its cradle and rubbed his eyes. He checked the rest of the third floor to ensure no one had overheard the short argument. All the makeshift cubicles were empty. Normally Kumar and Raju would have been in the office, but they hadn't returned from lunch yet.

Cosmo hadn't handled himself in the most godly manner during the heated conversation. He was glad the only apology he had to make was to God directly. Apologies aside, he still had to resolve the issue at hand.

He took the stairs several at a time and reached the lobby without encountering any of The Winning Team's staff or volunteers. Most of them were attending a local football match. Cosmo kicked open the back exit and stepped into the alley.

Waiting for him were two burly men dressed in suits. "I'm glad you chose to meet sooner rather than later. The issue we have to discuss is rather time sensitive, seeing how elections are next week."

"As I said over the phone," Cosmo's anger boiled quickly, "this conversation is not going to happen."

"It never happened." The spokesperson among the pair grinned.

Cosmo shook his head. "I'm not accepting money with strings attached. Donations only. No favors. No caveats."

The suit tapped the briefcase at his side. "You're the one who asked for the contribution. You know how the system works. My boss is already counting on your support."

"I asked for a charitable donation, for which I will account and provide detailed receipts."

"My boss isn't interested in receipts. He's interested in results."

Cosmo stood firm. "My results are plainly visible. Hundreds of volunteers serving thousands of children and young people every week."

"Those are not the sort of results my boss pays for, and you know it."

"I'm under no obligation to deliver any other kind." Cosmo stepped closer. His buttoned shirt and collar didn't reflect the wealth or connectedness of the suits. His trousers didn't speak of his fighting prowess. But his reputation spoke more loudly than any of those things.

These two men were clearly aware of Cosmo's reputation—one that demanded you came with a dozen men if you intended to make threats. The fact they'd come as a pair revealed the nature of their visit. "My boss will be disappointed you've chosen that stance."

"I'm sorry to hear that. I had hoped his giving to be motivated by charity rather than selfish gain."

Kumar and Raju rounded the corner as the suits turned to go.

The spokesman between the two suits laughed. "Everyone and everything is motivated by selfish gain. You should have learned that by now, Zimik."

"If that's how you feel, I suggest you keep your money and stop wasting my time." Cosmo got in the last words as the suits brushed past Kumar and Raju.

Kumar watched the suits disappear around the corner. "What's up?"

Cosmo didn't want to go into it. While disappointed at losing the money, mostly he was upset at being naive enough to think his old friends would give simply to improve their karma. "A potential donor wasn't satisfied with our results."

Raju stared back and forth between Kumar and Cosmo. "What do they want? A sermon from the gold medal stand at the World Cup? Maybe we could part the waters of the Bay of Bengal and walk across to Burma."

Cosmo shook his head. "They've got different ambitions than we do, less godly ones."

"Much less." Kumar added.

"Ah." Raju put the pieces together.

"It's nothing." Cosmo sighed. "We won't be bothered by them again."

"We won't be asking them for any more money, either." Kumar said.

"What about the budget for this year's Kenya Open?" Raju asked.

Cosmo gestured them inside. He opened the door and followed them up the stairs, talking as they went. "It's a big expense."

"Between the twelve players going, we know a dozen languages. We'll be able to counsel and share with players from all over India and parts of Asia." Raju built his case.

"I know." Cosmo reached the third floor. "I want the team to go. Even if we don't win like last year, it will be a great opportunity."

"And the money for the plane tickets?" Raju shifted papers on his desk.

Still standing at the top of the stairs, Cosmo pinched the bridge of his nose. "We'll find it. God will provide it somehow."

"And the rest?" Kumar asked.

"We'll have to trust God." Cosmo paced the room.

Kumar plopped down in a chair with a torn cushion. "We can't expect the team to sleep on the street and eat nothing but roasted dog."

"We still have a couple of weeks. I'll make some asks."

Kumar sighed. "It seems like only yesterday when we didn't have to make asks. The money just came in."

Raju slipped on a pair of sparring gloves. "I've had enough of the office for today. Kumar," he danced around jabbing the air, "how about you and I head down to the gym. It's time for some of our kids to show up."

"I wish I could." Kumar laced his hands behind his head.

Raju continued his shadow boxing directly in front of Kumar's face. "What's so important you can't work out for an hour?"

"I got a few more things to wrap up here."

"You've changed, bro." Raju tutted.

Kumar stood and shuffled toward his cubicle. "Half an hour, okay?"

"Fine, fine. I can find something to distract me for that long."

Fifteen minutes later, Cosmo started at a crashing sound from downstairs.

Kumar looked up. "That doesn't sound good."

"Thieves?" Raju rubbed his eyes, having fallen asleep at his desk.

Cosmo rushed to the window for a view of the street below. "Militants."

"What?" Kumar pulled a knife out from beneath his desk.

"Kumar." Cosmo nearly shouted as he rushed toward his compatriot. Instinctively, he batted the weapon out of Kumar's hand. "No weapons."

Kumar ground his teeth but made no effort to fetch the knife.

"Come on." Cosmo led the charge down the two flights of stairs. Their footsteps betrayed their arrival. By the time they reached the lobby, the last of the militants had fled through a broken window.

Raju pursued as far as the street corner.

Cosmo didn't have the heart. He surveyed the damage. In addition to the window, they'd broken down the front doors, smashed the lights and spattered cans of paint across the floor and walls.

His first thought was that he could have used the cans of paint. His next thought was that The Winning Team had suffered a losing season.

PART 6

OUT OF INDIA

Trip to Thailand

THE OVERHEAD LIGHT ILLUMINATED, indicating the plane's descent into Bangkok. Cosmo had felt the same downward momentum in the recent events of his life. During the first half of 1998, the opportunities had been endless. The last few months, not so much. He stretched to see over the seat back in front of him. Many of the passengers were asleep, the cabin dark.

Cosmo had remained awake during the entire red-eye flight from Delhi to Bangkok. Unable to sleep, he hadn't been able to focus either. His past had been so much easier to tolerate while his future overshadowed it. A hectic present wasn't enough by itself to crowd out past mistakes.

And his mistakes were many.

On top of asking for money from disreputable sources, Cosmo had unknowingly hired a government informant. Nine months of intelligence gathering had amounted to nothing more than a few charges of faulty accounting, disturbing the peace, public disorderliness and the illegal termination of stray dogs. Unfortunately, the incompetent spy had stolen the last of their money before disappearing.

The cabin lights rose halfway. The woman sleeping next to Cosmo stirred in her seat, turning her head in the other direction. Cosmo thanked God for small mercies. The woman's breath smelled of fish and the two single-serving bottles of Chardonnay she'd consumed over Burma. For the past thirty minutes she'd been breathing directly on him.

Cosmo shook off the bitterness he felt toward the informant. While the spy's betrayal had been the final straw, Cosmo had been responsible for the rest.

With Hindu militants seeking his life from north and south of Delhi, the risk to volunteers had skyrocketed. The need for security further crippled fundraising. In the end, Cosmo simply couldn't come up with the money.

Cosmo knew the scuttling of The Winning Team had been in everyone's best interest. He also knew he had let everyone down. If only he could have done things differently.

A flight attendant's voice broke the silence of the cabin, distracting Cosmo from his jumbled thoughts. The cabin lights rose to full intensity. Cosmo gazed out the window as the plane banked to his side. Bangkok's sprawl crept in every direction, groggy and dripping wet under an oppressive blanket of clouds.

He tried to muster excitement for Bangkok and the Asian Games. The World Sports Coalition's conference of sports ministry, held in tandem with the Asian Games, had provided him with a scholarship to serve as a volunteer minister.

The plane sailed into a cloud, blocking Cosmo's view. He settled into his seat. Perhaps with the conference and the games keeping his mind and body busy, he could untangle the spiritual mess beneath it all.

Introducing the New Girl

"TWO OLIVE GREEN DUFFLES." Cosmo planted his face into the palm of his hand and rested his elbow on the conference center counter. "Yes, they were labeled. Cosmo Zimik, Delhi to Bangkok, flight—"

The voice on the other end of the phone line cut him off.

He listened absently for several seconds. The words buzzing in his ear were rote. He'd heard the same lecture half a dozen times, at least once from the same nasally voice currently prattling on.

Tired of talking in circles, Cosmo resolved his bags were gone for good. "Thank you for your time." He hung up. He stretched and put his hands behind his head. The ornate wall clock behind the reception desk said 5:35pm. In two hours, the evening session of the sports ministry conference would begin.

He couldn't remember what tonight's topic was. Regret clouded his thinking. Unaccustomed to the feeling, Cosmo wasn't sure how to shake it.

He chided himself again for leaving The Winning Team floppy disk and three ring binder in his checked luggage. With those items gone, The Winning Team was truly dead. He had no other copy of the information: names and contact information for five hundred staff and volunteers from around the world, hundreds more donors, his best practices.

The last eighteen months of his life were lost, and he hadn't even any evidence they ever happened. Crossing the crowded lobby of the combined hotel and conference center, Cosmo sat at a table near a window. Reaching into the pocket of the neon-orange running suit his conference roommate had given him, he fetched one of his few remaining business cards—*It's time you join The Winning Team.*

He tossed the card on the table and stared out the window. The lush landscaping around the Catholic conference center and hotel reminded him of his Naga Hills—his Nagalim. It felt like he'd come full circle. Always scrapping to come out on top, the Naga remained permanently on the bottom.

Now that Cosmo thought about it, he couldn't be certain what team he'd been inviting people to join. When he had named his ministry, *The Winning Team*, it'd been a jab at everyone and everything he perceived as losing. Of course *his* team would win. But it hadn't. He had lost, again.

Even in the midst of his discouragement, he knew the idea to be ridiculous. The Winning Team was supposed to be God's team. Cosmo's failures hadn't changed that. His overreaching and impatience had toppled The Winning Team, but the people the ministry had impacted—they were still winning, weren't they?

"Excuse me. It's Cosmo, right?"

Cosmo blinked several times, breaking his trance-like gaze out the window. He turned toward an attractive brunette with an American accent. "Uh, yes." He stood. Instinctively, he bowed.

To his surprise she did as well—naturally, fluidly, and not as an afterthought like most Westerners. "My name's—"

"Sarah?"

She frowned. "How did you know?"

"Your name tag."

"Of course." Sarah gazed at her front where the tag clearly said, *Hello, my name is Sarah.*

Cosmo gestured toward the seat next to him. "Please, sit."

"Thank you."

Cosmo waited for Sarah to situate herself before retaking his own seat.

"Is this your ministry?" Sarah studied the business card Cosmo had tossed on the table.

He considered how to respond before deciding the truth would require less energy. "It was."

"Oh? You've started a new one?" She handed him the card.

"Not yet." Cosmo pocketed it.

Sarah studied him for a second, perhaps considering a follow up question to his cryptic remarks. "I was in the workshop you did on using martial arts to reach street kids in Asian slums."

"Really?" Cosmo perked up, happy to move the conversation away from his specific failures and toward his more general passion. "How did I miss you?"

Sarah blinked but didn't respond.

"I mean," Cosmo grinned, "I'm sure I would remember your face if I'd seen it."

Sarah raised a brow, no closer to responding to Cosmo's subtle flirting.

Cosmo decided not to push the matter further. "There aren't very many American women interested in martial arts."

"Oh, well." Sarah finally breathed out. "I might have been a bit late, so I had to sit in the back." She smiled, a radiant beam of a smile like a sun setting beneath an ocean horizon, and it knocked Cosmo off his guard.

Neither of them spoke for a long second until Cosmo gathered himself. "And what ministry are you involved in?"

"Me?" Sarah shrugged. "I teach children basketball and English as a platform to share about Jesus." Again she smiled wide, her teeth showing, a dimple on the right cheek, slight crinkles around her eye. She stopped speaking and Cosmo realized his gaze had been too intense.

He asked the first question to pop into his head. "Here in Thailand?"

She shook her head before diving into the work she'd been doing for the last few years in Hong Kong.

Cosmo listened to every word, feeling his passion rekindle from the heat of Sarah's. Their philosophies and goals were so similar.

Cosmo hadn't believed a woman or a westerner could share so many of his own ideas.

After several minutes, Sarah stopped abruptly. "But enough of me." She blushed lightly. "I'm not sure how you got me off on all that. I came over here to find out more about your martial arts ministry and how you think it could transfer to a place like Hong Kong."

Cosmo sighed. His heart sank and rose like ocean waves inside his chest. Months after terminating The Winning Team, he still hadn't allowed himself to fully grieve its loss. The need had pushed him to the verge of an emotional breakdown. And now here was Sarah, a sympathetic ear, a fellow worker, a kindred spirit. He wasn't sure how to begin.

Sarah stared at him, a quizzical look on her face.

"I'm not sure I'm the best person to ask."

Sarah laced her fingers and laid her hands on the table. "Oh? What makes you say that?" Her eyes softened. "You wouldn't be the first missionary to make a mistake."

Cosmo laughed. He'd never thought of himself as a missionary, not in the same sense Sarah used the word now.

"What's so funny?"

"Me as a missionary."

Sarah scrunched her brows. "Well, aren't you?"

"I guess I always thought of missionaries as foreigners with poor language skills."

Sarah laughed. "You mean like me."

Cosmo hemmed before granting a partial admission. "You've nailed the foreigner part, but to be honest, I haven't heard you speak anything but English. And you speak that pretty well."

"I should hope." Sarah rolled her eyes. "My English skills aside, I'm sure I fit the bill perfectly. My Cantonese is far from perfect. But enough avoiding the real issue." She breathed deeply. "What happened to The Winning Team?"

Without further dancing, Cosmo plowed into the matter directly. He shared the whole story from leaving Athletes in Action to closing The Winning Team offices. The only parts he held back were the threats from Hindu militants.

While he needed to unburden himself, there was only so much he could unload at once. And it seemed unfair to involve a total stranger with the seedy underbelly of Delhi's ongoing caste and religious warfare.

By the end of it, Sarah seemed dazed. "Wow."

Cosmo waited to see if she would push back her chair and flee.

She shook her head. "I knew India had to be an ethnically and religiously complex place, but I had no idea of the pressures Christians have to endure."

Cosmo relaxed. She wasn't going to bolt. "I'm sure many of the same pressures exist in Hong Kong."

"Maybe so." Sarah gazed out the window, as if she could see the hundreds of miles northeast to the peninsulas and islands of Hong Kong itself. "If so, they're difficult for an outsider to perceive. I'm sorry you had to go through all that." She returned her gaze to Cosmo.

He felt a hundred times lighter than he had an hour earlier. "Me too. I wish I wasn't such a slow learner. Maybe a good ministry would still be doing good things if I hadn't taken it out of God's hands. Hopefully the lesson won't be lost as well."

"I'm sure it won't be, not after what I've just heard and the way you shared it." Sarah said.

"Oh?"

"It takes humility to be so blunt about your failures."

Cosmo nodded as he stood. He glanced at the clock behind the receptions desk. "Have you had dinner?"

Sarah shook her head.

"The dining room's serving for thirty minutes still. I wasn't hungry before. Suddenly I feel the need to eat several small animals."

"Yikes." Sarah stood.

Cosmo gave her a wary eye. "You're not a vegetarian, are you?"

"Heaven's no. I just hope the animals are cooked first."

Cosmo shrugged. "If not, we can always start a fire out back."

"In this humidity?"

"I grew up in the jungle."

"Really? I suppose that's something to talk about over dinner." Side by side, the two hurried toward the dining room. When they arrived, delegates were streaming out, in a hurry to sneak in a shower or a nap before the evening session.

"Oh, another thing we could discuss." Cosmo stood aside so Sarah could enter through the crowded doorway first.

"What's that?"

"I was wondering if you might want some volunteer help to get your martial arts program going in Hong Kong."

Hong Kong Courtship

COSMO HELD OPEN THE door to the restaurant he'd chosen for his and Sarah's night out. Their first official date had occurred during Cosmo's first extended stay in Hong Kong. This evening marked the third month of his second visit.

Neatly stenciled across the glass door, the establishment's name read, THAI DELIGHT, all in caps. The location had been what sold him, not the name.

The sixth-floor restaurant sat within sight of Victoria Harbor and overlooked the Expo Promenade. He'd decided the restaurant had to be Thai, based on the fact they first met in Bangkok. THAI DELIGHT had been the only Thai restaurant on Hong Kong Island with a view and even remotely close to his price range.

They continued their friendly yet awkward discourse while waiting to be shown to their table. Finally Sarah burst out. "When were you planning on telling me how the TV spot went today?"

Cosmo grinned. He'd avoided the hot topic of the day in hopes of achieving such an outburst. "Oh, that? I can hardly remember."

She punched him in the arm.

He didn't bother pretending it hurt. She knew better. The hostess returned to show them to a relatively isolated table pushed against a window that spanned an entire wall of the restaurant.

Cosmo pulled Sarah's chair out, scooted her in, took his own seat and promptly spread the menu in front of his face.

Sarah plucked it from his hands.

"I was reading that."

"The wine list?"

Cosmo glanced again at the menu he had picked up. "The prices are outrageous. I don't know how people afford to both drink and eat."

"Good thing neither of us drink." Sarah glared at him.

Finally Cosmo cracked. "Okay, I'll talk. Why don't you at least look at the menu. I'm starving."

"No small animals this time."

"Unless it's a chicken."

Sarah conceded. "Chicken is fine. Although I'm sorta in the mood for tofu."

Cosmo twitched, exaggerating his disgust.

"Just tell me about the interview. What did they ask about? Is it going to be on the news tonight?" She pretended to look at the menu while waiting for his response.

As Cosmo watched her watching him, he relived his disbelief over how the interview at the television station had gone. "It really couldn't have gone any better. I'm still surprised how much the people here are shocked by the association of Christianity and martial arts. They kept returning to my religious beliefs, which kept giving me chances to share the Gospel."

Sarah gave up the pretense of looking at the menu. "You shared the whole Gospel? And they filmed it?"

"Probably three different times. I'm not sure they even recognized what I was saying." Cosmo shrugged. "It should be great exposure for the program. I bet we get a dozen new recruits by this weekend."

"You don't think they'll be turned off?" Sarah asked.

"I bet they'll be even more curious."

The waiter began his approach.

Sarah buried her face in the menu.

The waiter retreated to give them more time.

Cosmo took the opportunity to browse his own menu. Forget tofu. He was in the mood for beef curry. Soon the waiter returned, and Cosmo ordered for both of them. No tofu.

They enjoyed a comfortable meal and easy conversation that

roamed from topics of sports ministry to the current relationship between Hong Kong and China. Before the waiter could return to ask about dessert, something Cosmo knew Sarah would decline, Cosmo worked himself up for his endgame.

Their ministry partnership so far had been based on directness. Their friendship naturally flowed out of their shared passion for the ministry. In Cosmo's mind, anything less than a lifetime commitment to explore their passion together seemed ridiculous.

Their eventual marriage was a foregone conclusion. Tonight was the night to make their intentions official. Cosmo spoke suddenly. "I have given it many hours of thought and prayer."

Sarah returned her gaze from the glittering lights of Victoria Harbor to the excited look on Cosmo's face.

"Even though we have not known each other long, I know I love you," he said.

The corners of Sarah's mouth turned upward, stopping short of a full smile. She blinked then opened her mouth as if to speak. No response came.

Cosmo continued. "God told me I am supposed to marry you."

The hint of a smile on Sarah's face disappeared, her mouth still slightly open.

During the awkward silence, the waiter swept past the table and deposited the check. He didn't ask about dessert.

Cosmo slipped enough cash into the folder and nudged it to the edge of the table. He looked up at Sarah and smiled. "What do you think?"

"Um." She finally closed her mouth and swallowed. "Well, God hasn't told me I'm supposed to marry you."

Cosmo frowned.

Sarah continued. "So, I guess I'll pray about it and get back to you."

Cosmo nodded. Perhaps he had gotten in front of the matter again. He thought he understood Sarah, but it was possible he moved too quickly for people as well as God. "Sounds good."

Cosmo's father had long preached the value of humility. Intentionally or not, Sarah now emphasized patience. One thing Cosmo knew for sure, Sarah was worth the time and effort. Even if he had to burn a trail between Delhi and Hong Kong, he'd convince her to share their future.

Seven trips and over three years later, Cosmo would finally succeed.

Meeting the Family

AT SARAH'S REQUEST, COSMO touched down at LAX first. The plan was to meet her parents before embarking on a fundraising campaign to launch a new ministry. The two of them had known each other for less than a year and had been dating for only a couple months. Cosmo hadn't asked Sarah a second time to marry him, but he planned on doing so after his fundraising trip.

First, he would meet his future in-laws. After stepping off the plane, he shouldered his duffle and headed straight for passenger pickup. Bangkok had taught Cosmo a lesson: carry on all luggage.

When he had asked Sarah if he should wait until she could introduce him directly to her family, she had insisted everything would be fine. Besides, she intended to remain in Hong Kong for another year.

Cosmo navigated the busy terminal and stepped through the automatic doors leading to the ground-level pick up area for arrivals. Summer in Los Angeles was easily five degrees cooler than Delhi and less humid than Hong Kong.

Cosmo glanced up and down the row of idling vehicles. All he knew to look for was a white Chevy Cavalier. None of the waiting cars matched the description.

As he scanned the travelers milling around him, he realized he would be easy to spot. A nearby family of Hispanic origin came the closest in skin color, but no one in all of Asia would mistake them as *bahadur*.

Cosmo mused at a row of shiny, yellow taxis neatly awaiting

customers. In Delhi, multiple autowallahs would have either solicited or insulted him by now.

Finally a taxi driver approached him. "Where to, buddy?"

Cosmo shook his head. "I'm waiting to meet my future mother-in-law."

Confused, the driver made an act of scanning the nearby crowd. "Shouldn't you be looking for your future wife first? Or do they do things differently where you come from?"

Cosmo grinned. "Maybe a little. The future wife is in Hong Kong."

"And she sent you alone?"

Cosmo nodded as a white sedan that fit the bill approached. "She's still making up her mind."

"In that case, I'll repeat my offer. Where to, pal?"

"Thanks anyway, but I think my ride is here." Cosmo pointed with his chin as the white Cavalier angled into a spot a dozen meters away.

"Good luck then. You got cojones. I'll give you that much." The driver winked as he dissolved into the crowd to look for a fare.

Cosmo wasn't sure what cojones meant. Based on the context, he could guess. If correct, he knew he had cojones. But he couldn't figure out why his current situation required them.

A middle-aged woman, about Cosmo's height, exited the driver's seat of the car he had been watching. As she rounded the front bumper, she eyed Cosmo. "Cosmo Zimik?"

Cosmo puffed his chest and softened his expression. "Mrs. Lang, it is so nice to meet you." He rushed forward, lowered his bags and bowed.

The woman didn't return the gesture. "It's nice to meet you. Sarah has spoken enthusiastically." She waited for Cosmo to straighten. "There's room for your things in the trunk." As she spoke, the trunk mechanically popped open.

Cosmo realized another woman in the passenger side front seat had released it. Sweeping his bags into the trunk, he closed it and reached the driver side door before Sarah's mother. He opened the door for her and stood back.

The woman hesitated. Her hair, while thinning slightly, held its dark, iron wood coloring. Perhaps a little softer around the edges than most Naga women her age, she preserved a degree of determination Cosmo appreciated at once. She sat behind the wheel and Cosmo closed her door.

While dropping into the back seat, Cosmo mulled over the possibility these two middle-aged, white women were not in fact Sarah's family, but instead hired by one of his enemies to secret him away to a remote location. It was a plot worthy of Bollywood.

The woman in the front passenger seat turned to introduce herself. "Nice to meet you, Cosmo. I'm Sarah's aunt."

Cosmo shook her hand. "Nice to meet you, Mrs.—"

"Nolen."

"Mrs. Nolen." Cosmo repeated her name.

She turned front and tapped Sarah's mother on the arm. "You've got an opening after this van."

Mrs. Lang nodded. After the van passed, she stepped on the accelerator hard and lurched into the flow of traffic. The introductions were put on hold as the two women navigated their way back onto the interstate heading north.

As the car merged, Cosmo broke the silence. "I'm glad it worked out that I could visit my in-laws before the marriage."

"Oh?" Sarah's aunt turned to face Cosmo. Her smile quickly faded. "Wait." She blinked several times, then looked at her sister. "Christi, did you know about this?"

"No." Mrs. Lang shook her head. "I mean, there's nothing to know. Sarah hasn't said a thing."

Cosmo cut in. "We haven't set the date yet, if that's what you are wondering. I only meant to say, it will be better that I meet Sarah's family before I take her to the jungle to meet mine."

Mrs. Nolen's eyes widened. "Take her to the jungle?"

Cosmo nodded. "To meet my people. After Sarah and I are married we will minister to them."

Sarah's mother gripped the wheel, her knuckles white. "For

goodness sake! Married and living in the jungle? You've only known each other for a handful of months."

The aunt soothed the mother. "Calm down. I'll handle this." Without preamble, Mrs. Nolen shot straight to the point. "Cosmo, how do you expect to support Sarah? I mean, how do you plan to put food on the table as a missionary, if you don't mind me asking."

Cosmo thought about the question for a few seconds. Images of his own family sharing meager meals flashed through his mind. Times had changed. Cosmo was not his father. "With God's help I've provided food enough for hundreds of children in Delhi slums on multiple occasions. I've fed literally thousands of people in India. Sarah is only one skinny American woman. Feeding her will not be a challenge."

The car fell silent. Despite Cosmo's level response, he sensed the two women were upset at him. Obviously Sarah had not broached the topic of marriage with her family. But his traveling the globe to see them should have been some indication of his seriousness. He had expected them to be excited about the news.

The aunt continued the questioning without turning around in her seat. "How many people have you beat up, Cosmo?" Her tone indicated she meant the question quite seriously.

Cosmo blinked. Direct was one thing. This was another. She hadn't even asked *if* he had beaten anyone, or under what circumstance, but how many. Cosmo laughed it off without answering. Either Sarah had underestimated her family's resistance to him, or Cosmo had chosen the wrong approach.

Maybe he had a thing or two to learn still, but what was done was done. He sighed. The next day and a half in Hemet, California were going to be long ones. Cosmo knew courting Sarah would require all his patience. He had hoped he wouldn't need to court her family as well. *Patience*, Cosmo repeated the word to himself.

Meeting the Family, Part Two

UNLIKE WHEN COSMO HAD first traveled between Manipur and Delhi, flights now made the round trip twice weekly. Normally, Cosmo would have taken a train, but he wanted Sarah's first visit to his home village to be as comfortable as possible. While she was accustomed to traveling throughout Asia, Cosmo feared his jungle might be a shock.

By the time they stepped off the plane in Imphal, the chilly January day had risen to a comfortable 19 degrees Celsius with the sun shining overhead. Cosmo checked on Sarah through the corner of his eye. She hugged his arm and smiled.

Cosmo knew his years of patience were nearing a happy ending. It had been over two years since he'd met Sarah in November of 1998 at the Asian Games in Bangkok. She hadn't said yes to him yet, but only formalities remained. In a few minutes she would meet his parents.

They took their time progressing from the tarmac to the pick up area. Parked across the street, in the shade, Cosmo spotted his parents in a rented Jeep.

Sarah shivered and squeezed Cosmo's arm to her side.

Cosmo plunged into the traffic, towing Sarah with him. They worked their way steadily across the busy street. "They'll be so proud I've chosen someone so special."

"Stop it. You're making me blush."

"I mean it. You are not like any other woman. They will recognize that."

Sarah narrowed her eyes at Cosmo and scrutinized him. "You're not like any other guy I've met either."

They reached the far curb. Cosmo winked. "I know. So much talent and humility in such a handsome package." Before Sarah could respond, he tugged her toward the Jeep while waving to his parents.

His father climbed out of the Jeep and hurried to open the door for Cosmo's mother. The four of them met on the sidewalk beside the Jeep.

Cosmo bowed to his father and hugged his mother. "Mom, Dad, this is Sarah."

Sarah bowed. She shook hands with Cosmo's father.

Cosmo's mother stepped forward to take Sarah's hand in her own. She smiled while gazing deeply into Sarah's eyes. A few seconds passed without another word—only the comfort and warmth of a family glad to see a son and gain a daughter.

"Come." Cosmo's father gestured toward the Jeep. He helped his wife into the back seat where Cosmo and Sarah joined her. Lastly, Cosmo's father took the front seat next to the driver.

After a bumpy three-hour ride, they arrived at Cosmo's village. He breathed deeply of the fresh air and turned to Sarah. "Remember, there's no electricity. So everything is done a bit differently."

"It's beautiful, really." Sarah breathed the words reverently.

"Thank you. I think so." The Jeep pulled to a stop and Cosmo jumped out to pay the driver. He tipped him generously. "Return here next Wednesday morning."

The driver smiled and gave the thumbs up while driving away.

"This way." Cosmo took Sarah's hand.

"Where are we going first?"

The two couples were already drawing curious stares from other villagers. Cosmo didn't know them, so he smiled and kept walking. "I couldn't introduce you to parts of my family first, while leaving out others, so—"

"Don't say it." Sarah interrupted.

Cosmo shrugged. "It's only family. And extended family. Well, some of them aren't technically family. Family is a loose term in the village." The couple stopped in front of a large hut and allowed Cosmo's parents to go ahead.

"In there?" Sarah asked. "So it's a party."

"More like a family meal."

"Please tell me you didn't invite the whole village." Sarah said.

"I didn't invite anyone. My sister took care of that."

"Alright Cosmo Zimik, lead the way." She looped her arm through his.

Cosmo stood his ground. "First, I need to know how to introduce you."

Sarah raised a brow. "By my name?"

"I was referring to your title. I don't want anyone in the village getting the wrong idea about our chasteness."

Sarah suppressed a smirk. "Then shouldn't you be asking me something? A certain traditional question?"

Cosmo stood back and shook his head. "I've asked you a dozen times already."

"But I've never said yes."

Cosmo clamped his jaw shut. Sarah had won this one. The fact only strengthened Cosmo's confidence that she could balance his extremes. He looked her in the eyes. For what he hoped would be the last time, he asked her the same question he had asked every few months for the past two years. "Sarah Lang, will you be my wife?"

Sarah wrapped her arms around him and smiled victoriously. "Yes."

Cosmo squeezed her once, then stepped back. He cleared his throat. "Chasteness. We mustn't forget."

The door cracked open. A woman about Cosmo's age stuck her head out before ducking back inside. "She's beautiful!" The woman reappeared, a huge smile on her face. She threw the door open and hugged Cosmo.

After a few seconds, Cosmo introduced her. "Sarah, this is my sister, Vasty."

The next few minutes were a whirlwind of introductions, bows, and handshakes until eventually Cosmo and Sarah found themselves seated at the head of a table of all men.

Sarah leaned close to Cosmo's ear. "Where are the women?"

"In the village it is traditional for guests and men to eat first."

Sarah scanned the room again. "But I'm the only woman. It's weird."

"It's village tradition." Cosmo looked at his finally fiancé and decided to break the tradition. "Okay, wait here." He disappeared into the kitchen.

Sarah heard the conversation through the thin wall, but it was in Cosmo's native tongue.

After a few minutes, Cosmo's sisters dragged extra chairs to the table and sat.

Cosmo emerged with his mother. He insisted she take the seat right next to his. Cosmo couldn't be sure, but he thought he saw a smile on his father's face.

After a few quiet moments of serving food and eating, the mood around the table returned to a jovial one. Cosmo squeezed Sarah's hand. Their first dinner as a promised couple was a perfect combination of their two cultures. And his family was fuller than ever. Cosmo leaned toward his mother. "She's wonderful, isn't she?"

Cosmo's mother cracked a smile. "I'm proud of you, son. You have chosen wisely."

Two hours later, Cosmo found himself surprisingly alone with his father. Sarah had requested space to be with her journal. The rest of Cosmo's family were either cleaning up the afternoon meal, or preparing for breakfast the next morning. As a result, his parent's hut fell quiet.

Sitting on the weathered and repeatedly repaired bench attached to the back, Cosmo and his father appreciated a restful silence. Nothing in Hong Kong or Delhi came close to the quiet of the jungle. Countless sounds were still there, but they required attentiveness and focus to discern them.

The sun was still up. The temperature had peaked at a perfect 26 degrees Celsius. Cosmo closed his eyes and soaked in the moment.

Finally, he asked his father a question he'd been wanting to ask for several months. "How do you keep doing it, year after year? How do you know what decisions to make next? Which steps to take?"

Seconds passed, carried away on a subtle breeze.

Cosmo's father turned to face him. "You want to know the secret, son? The only secret I've learned?"

Cosmo nodded.

"Seek God deeper." His father exhaled and stared across the village to the edge of the jungle beyond. "Whenever you find yourself lost in life, it is the only answer. Seek God deeper."

Cosmo let his father's words sink in. They were not the words of a university-educated man, but of a God educated man. So much made sense in light of those words. Cosmo understood his father better because of them. "That's all you've ever done, isn't it?"

"I've tried. It hasn't always been easy. Even the best men are entangled by religion and the work bound up with it. This is my only advice, son. Do not seek the ministry. Seek God deeper."

Cosmo felt chains fall from his wrists. Layers of resentment melted from around his heart. Through all the lean years of his childhood, when every force of man had pressured his father to give up, he had continued faithfully seeking God.

His father had not sought success. He had not sought compensation. He had not sought power or acclaim, even though Cosmo was convinced he could have achieved them all. Instead he had chosen only to seek God deeper. And because of that, he had attained a quiet strength Cosmo had striven for his whole life, but never come close to achieving.

"I'm sorry, Dad." A burden lifted from Cosmo's shoulders—one he had not realized he still carried.

"For what?"

"For blaming you. I'm sorry it has taken me this long to understand."

Bumpy Spell

SARAH PACED THE LIVING room of her parents' ranch style house. "It isn't the job situation that has me worried." She turned to face the couch where Cosmo sat. The lights in the room had remained off during the sunny afternoon. Now that the sun had sunk low in the western sky, the room became dark.

"It's your family," Cosmo said.

"We've been in California for six months and things aren't getting any easier. We've only two months until our wedding, and you're not even trying."

"They've made up their mind. What else is there for me to do?"

"You could be friendly." Sarah huffed.

"The first thing your aunt asked me was how many people I've beaten. There is no friendly response to that." Cosmo kept his cool.

Sarah stamped her foot. "I've already apologized for that. And besides, you always just assume everything is going to happen the way you see it. You never give anyone else a chance to participate. Things might have turned out differently if you would have asked my parents permission to marry me or at least waited more than two months after our first date to bring it up."

"I was unfamiliar with the tradition."

"That's another thing." Sarah deflated. "This is a different world than the jungle. It's hard for my family to understand."

Cosmo stood. "They do not want to understand."

"I didn't understand until you took me to the jungle. To them, it's all just crazy stories—"

Cosmo shook his head and held up a hand to stop his fiancé from continuing the same well-trodden path. "The next two months won't do anything to change that."

"Then maybe we should postpone the wedding." Sarah turned away.

Cosmo held his breath. He hadn't expected the argument to come to this. One thing the last three years of courting Sarah had taught him was she did not appreciate being pressured.

He exhaled. "If that is what you want, I can give you space. I'll move and we'll postpone the wedding. But none of this changes my belief we shall be married." The room had grown almost completely dark. Cosmo couldn't tell if Sarah had begun crying or not.

Her voice quivered. "That's what I'm talking about. You don't even care about anyone else's process. You've already made up your mind."

"I made up my mind three years ago. I don't know how to unmake it now. That doesn't mean I don't care."

Sarah remained quiet.

"How long?"

"How long what?" Sarah whispered.

"How much time apart do you need?" For the first time during the conversation, Cosmo's heart sank. As he spoke the word 'apart' aloud, the reality of how dire their relationship had become settled in his gut.

"Six months." Sarah's voice grew stronger. "We should take six months apart."

Cosmo strode toward the entryway.

Sarah almost hailed him. Before she could, Cosmo stopped.

He turned to face her and bowed. "Tell your family I said goodbye. I love you."

"I—" Sarah choked on her words.

"I know. See you in six months." Cosmo let himself out. He stood in the driveway as the day's dying light fled beneath the horizon. His chest constricted at the thought of spending another six months without his fiancé.

He opened his car door and plopped in the driver's seat. Before starting the '93 Corolla, he determined to return to the northwest. Perhaps Bend, Oregon. He had spent some time there raising money. Or Idaho. He had a friend outside of Boise who had offered to mentor him in residential construction. The Rocky Mountains comforted him.

When life in Delhi had gotten too dangerous, Sarah had offered to sponsor Cosmo's coming to the United States. At the time, the move had seemed obvious. But living near Sarah's family had taken a toll.

The more he thought about getting away to Idaho, the more at peace he felt. "Idaho it is." He started the car and backed out of the drive.

Idaho Calm

COSMO CIRCULATED AMONG THE half-dozen students in his makeshift class. Boise's Ann Morrison Park created as ideal a location for martial arts instruction as any park in Delhi, plus no one ever fought over the space. Cosmo corrected a young man's side kick, then realized multiple people were making the same mistake.

Using a tree trunk, Cosmo demonstrated the correct form before having the students circle the tree and try it themselves. They were a motley crew: a college student, a young mother with her baby sleeping in a nearby stroller stuffed with blankets, a man who always seemed to be in the park.

Since Cosmo hadn't officially received his work permit yet, the group offered impromptu donations to help keep him fed. Cosmo praised the group's improvement. As they struck the large trunk from all sides, a smattering of leaves drifted from its branches—less due to their kicking and more due to the chill October weather.

He noted a police cruiser crawling along the road that bisected the park but didn't think anything of it. Police in the United States, outside of airport security and customs, had never given Cosmo any trouble.

Moments later, two officers approached the class on foot. "Excuse me, sir. Are you the instructor here?"

Cosmo faced the pair with a smile. "Yes, officers. Can I help you?"

"Do you have a permit for instructing martial arts or for conducting a performance in the park?"

Cosmo shook his head. "We're just practicing."

The second officer wandered toward the incongruous group of students. "Are any of you paying this man for his instruction?"

In unison the group shook their heads no. The college student spoke up. "We just come out here to practice. This guy was nice enough to offer us some tips."

The officer eyed the student suspiciously. "You don't pay him for those tips?"

"No, sir." The student stood his ground. Donations weren't officially the same as payments.

The first officer took over. "Paid or not, you can't host a class of any sort in the park without a permit."

"I'm sorry, officer. I was not aware." Cosmo wondered if someone had seen him and his class knocking bark off the tree and decided to call the police. It certainly wasn't anything worth arguing about.

"You're not in any sort of trouble, this time. Just a verbal warning." The officer and Cosmo stared at each other for a few seconds without flinching. The officer seemed confused by the fact that Cosmo neither demonstrated malice or fear. "But you'll need to be moving along."

Cosmo nodded. He bowed toward his class.

They bowed in return.

Without further words, they gathered their stuff from piles on the grass and parted ways, each heading in a different direction.

Cosmo checked briefly on the sleeping baby tucked beneath a layer of blankets. He smiled at its mother before strolling toward the river.

He didn't want to push his luck, but if he judged the police correctly, they were indifferent about breaking up his class. He figured it should be safe enough to return to a different section of the park in a couple of days—weather permitting.

Every morning at the same time, he walked from his apartment, located on the upper bench section of Boise, down to the park. Casually, he started his workout routine at 9am. That way if people wanted to join him, they always knew when. And an Asian man performing martial arts in Boise was never too hard to find, even in a park the size of Ann Morrison.

He reached a footpath on the edge of the river and followed it west, downstream, toward the section of the greenbelt people had comically warned him to avoid. Boise residents' ideas about what constituted dangerous amused him. He supposed it a good thing they hadn't been exposed to the sorts of dangers he had taken for granted both in the jungle village and the corrupt streets of Delhi.

As he strolled beneath the mottled light and shadow of large cottonwood trees, he focused on replacing the noises of the city with the gurgling of the Boise River and the crunch of leaves beneath his feet. Even after a mild confrontation with local police, Cosmo had never felt so peaceful.

No one sought to take his life. No threat of assault hovered around him. He hadn't carried a knife or short section of pipe as weapons in months.

He genuinely liked his life in Idaho, even if it felt like a delay in fulfilling his true purpose of bringing economic sustainability to jungles and rural villages all over the world.

He had found a local church that allowed him to teach informal martial arts classes. The classes gave him a platform for sharing his story. On Saturdays he often held demonstrations at the skate park where he shared his faith with kids from all over town. Never had anyone threatened him for talking about Jesus.

He missed Sarah, but the six months were nearly up.

During their separation, Sarah had decided at her own pace the two of them were meant to be together. They had already agreed on a new wedding date.

He left the footpath and perched himself on top a sunny rock. Closing his eyes, he filtered the smell of decaying leaves and goose manure from the urban odors. Not exactly the jungle of Nagalim, it soothed him nonetheless.

In six weeks, Cosmo would travel back to California and marry Sarah in the spring of 2002 rather than the fall of 2001. Then the two of them would move to Idaho. Sarah would love the tranquility of Idaho as much as he did. Boise would serve as a great place to honeymoon while waiting for Cosmo's green card.

Together they'd be free to resume the ministry they felt called to pursue. Months and years from now, they would look back at this time in Idaho as a wonderful sabbatical. Nothing more.

Idaho Desert

"WE SIMPLY CAN'T AFFORD to keep two chaplains on staff."

"And the rising inmate population?" Cosmo asked.

"It's because of the rising inmate population." Cosmo's supervisor at Idaho State Correctional Institution pressed her hand against the side of her face in an effort to wipe away the weariness shown there. "I realize its counter intuitive. But with the economy in the crapper and everyone focused on terrorism abroad, there's barely enough money to pay the bills and keep the prisoners fed."

Cosmo nodded. He understood this was as close to an apology as his supervisor was going to give. The more he thought about it, the more he realized an apology wasn't necessary. He had been a great chaplain, but the position did not define him. "Don't worry about it."

She raised a brow, puzzled by Cosmo's statement.

"I've worked six good years here, much longer than I had planned. The time has given me direction. I think getting laid off is part of God's timing. There's been a venture I've wanted to start. Maybe this is the time to start it."

His supervisor sighed. "Thank you for your understanding and your years of dedicated service." She smiled. It was a tired expression, but a genuine one.

Cosmo stood, pushing back his chair. "Thank you. I've enjoyed the opportunity."

His supervisor stood as well. She extended her hand across the desk.

Cosmo shook it and then bowed before exiting the small office for the last time.

Outside, he breathed in the country air. His office had been in Kuna, Idaho, a rural settlement south of Boise. Acquiring the job had been a blessing, considering his lack of green card until a year ago. Cosmo strode toward his GMC Sierra in the parking lot.

The supposed six-month process of obtaining the green card had taken six long years. Cosmo had assumed the moment he obtained the card, Sarah and he would cut loose from Idaho and return to Asia.

Now that travel was legal, God held them back. Perhaps it was still too dangerous for Cosmo to return to India. Now he had Sarah to protect. Maybe, Cosmo wondered, God had a lesson for him here in Idaho—a lesson he had yet to learn.

He sat in his truck with the motor running, the transmission in park. He rested his head on the steering wheel. Despite his personal longing to return home to Nagalim, he couldn't escape the burden he felt for the young men he had met in Idaho's correctional facilities. Often times, the inmates' children were already repeating the mistakes of their fathers.

In hospital rooms, courtrooms and prison cells, he'd witnessed their utter aloneness. No parents, no teachers, no chance. From his work the past six years, he knew Canyon County, the neighboring county to the west, contained the highest percentage of at risk youth anywhere in Idaho. The numbers were higher than much of the Western United States.

With its depressed economy, migratory workforce and rampant gangs, the opportunities for kids to go bad abounded. The circumstances were a far cry from growing up in Cosmo's village. Few of Idaho's teens were in danger of starving or having their homes burned by government authorities. But Cosmo had loving parents. These kids had no one.

At a gut level, Cosmo connected with their plight. He recognized their anger and lack of trust. He understood their impulse to fight. They reminded him of himself.

For several months his gut had prompted him to do something

about it—to open his own dojo, a martial arts gym for kids who had nowhere else to go. His current lack of a job would give him plenty of time. His cashed in pension would give him the money.

Still, Cosmo resisted the idea, aware that a dojo would tie him down. While the thought of living in Idaho for a short respite had been romantic, the seven-plus years Cosmo had lived there felt more like a prison sentence with no foreseeable end.

He shifted the truck into drive and headed for home. If Sarah confirmed his inclination, they'd do it together. They would do it for every individual kid taken off the streets.

Instead of trying to teach them not to fight, he'd show them the difficult path to becoming a true warrior: discipline, strength, courage, humility and surrender. Cosmo would teach them to fight for something beyond themselves.

During the thirty-minute commute from the prison to his home, Cosmo realized these five pillars constituted the lessons his father and Mark had tried to teach him. Discipline, strength, courage, humility and surrender. His whole life, God had hammered the pillars home.

Surrender had been the final pillar of his education. Only now did Cosmo recognize the truth. It had taken years of having his personal plans and ambitions thwarted—The Winning Team, his attempts to marry Sarah, his plans to bring economic reform to rural Asia. He had learned at last to honor God's plans over his own.

Taken together, the pillars enabled Cosmo to stop grasping and scrapping and taking. From the jungle to the streets to the countryside of Idaho, it had taken Cosmo many miles and many years to learn the lessons every Naga would need to become a true warrior.

Idaho farmland slid past on both sides of the truck. The fields were not all that different from the ones of Cosmo's youth. The crops were not the same, but the people who grew them shared much in common. Their desires were the same.

Cosmo worshipped a God who longed to give humans the exact things they strove to take. But only open, empty hands could receive. Cosmo knew the name he would give the dojo, if he and Sarah decided to open it—Empty Hand Combat.

EPILOGUE:

In Cosmo's Own Words

The View From Nampa, Idaho

I AM NOT A writer, so I've partnered with David Mark Brown to bring you my story in a manner that will hopefully connect much more than if I had written it myself. But I want to take a moment to let you know why the story has been written in the first place, and where I believe God is leading me from here.

This book is based on both my journey and my dream. Yes, I still feel God has set it in my heart to bring freedom to third world countries through the implementation of reproducible, self-sustaining economic practices. I never imagined my journey toward realizing that dream would go through Idaho.

Growing up amidst the spirits of poverty and fear, I have witnessed more than my fair share of discrimination and hate from loan sharks, militants, and armies. I've witnessed injustices too numerous to list—everything from the killing of family members to the harassment of helpless widows.

Even as a child, I thought to myself, *when I grow up, I am going to bring justice and freedom to the jungle.* I determined to rid our small tribes of fear, power mongers and poverty. My whole life has been dedicated to that singular passion. Although, as my story reveals, I've not always known the best way to achieve it.

Then came a series of trials of a different sort.

Starting in 2010, I found myself spiritually burdened and financially broke beyond anything I had previously imagined. To do something good for cast out and hurting children, I started a small martial arts gym.

Sarah and I used our savings, including my retirement from working for the Idaho Prisons. We used the money hoping to prosper and bloom beyond Idaho and eventually facilitate my dream of self-sustaining villages throughout the jungles of Asia.

The opposite happened, and we didn't prosper financially. Broken and humbled, I cried out to God. The word that came into my heart was the same word my Dad had spoken to me right before he passed away in 2002—"Seek God deeper."

That was when my approach toward life radically changed. I finally realized I didn't have to change the whole world, but just the world around me—one step at a time. I needed to nurture the people around me and start the Empty Hand Revolution one person at a time, just like my father, and mentors like Mark, did with me. In the long run, the multiplicative ripple effect from those individuals will be larger than any splash I make on my own.

Along those lines, I am mentoring youth and young adults in America through my gym and ministry, Empty Hand Combat. A partner foundation, Empty Hand Warrior, provides scholarship money for children who cannot afford instruction. At the same time, Sarah and I are raising warriors in the jungles of Asia by funding their education and supporting orphanages.

The Morung Project

MY EMBRACING OF THE Empty Hand Revolution has only strengthened my resolve to create a reproducible model of economic self-sustainability for rural villages across the third world. This effort has birthed The Morung Project.

Two hundred years ago, every Naga village huddled around a Morung. The Morung was where elders trained young men to become warriors. They left their homes and temporarily lived in the Morung. They studied, they hunted, they trained for combat.

In modern times, the Morung has become a concept among the Naga. It binds Nagas together and represents the positive aspects of our culture. The Morung Project shares similar aims. It is my fervent prayer, that by dispelling poverty and fear, The Morung Project can restore freedom and justice to shattered rural villages not just in my Nagalim, but throughout the third world.

With empty hands, I am finally starting this work with one of the smallest tribes in India,—the Tarao. I've chosen this most humble tribe for three reasons:

1.) I have no strings attached to Tarao tribe—no blood relatives, and no friends.

2.) Tarao tribe is the poorest tribe in all of India.

3.) Tarao tribe is one of the smallest tribes in Southeast Asia.

I have chosen the smallest and poorest tribe to launch The Morung Project, because that is how God's Kingdom works. The last shall be first. The Good News of Jesus the Christ is always accepted first among the least, the lost and the losers.

The new revolution and the regeneration that the Naga seek (and that most human beings seek) will rise only through God and his grace. In the mind-boggling words of Jesus, "The meek shall inherit the earth."

Since all Nagas are part of this small and meek tribe, all Nagas will be able to bear testimony to the world that God has generated new life from the Tarao. And all the world will see that glorious life can sprout from the lowliest of places. Beyond the Tarao tribe, I hope the world will see all Nagas sincerely seeking God deeper and testifying of his glory in our daily walk of life.

From northeast India, I hope the The Morung Project will spread.

The plight of Tarao tribe is a common one known around the world. After The Morung Project generates success stories of economic, cultural and spiritual regeneration among the Naga, I hope the model will be reproduced. I hope others will do even more than this as they constantly seek God deeper.

To find out more, visit: http://www.morungproject.com.

Welcome to the Empty Hand Revolution

SARAH AND I, AND those partnering with us, don't intend to recruit the world to join our personal ministry or mission. Instead, we want others to replicate our ideas (steal them and claim them as your own!) so the concept of the Empty Hand Revolution can multiply.

We want to hold everything loosely and own nothing, in the same manner my father reflected through his life. A story is told of my father about how he longed to no longer bear the label of ordained pastor within the Baptist denomination. He had tired so thoroughly that when church leaders approached him about his uncomfortable (and charismatic) tendencies to heal the sick, he happily resigned.

To his displeasure, God confronted him about the resignation and convicted him to reenlist. The denomination took him back without their previous restrictions. In this same way, I have built precautions within the ministry goals of The Morung Project against controlling and grasping hands. The work is nothing about me and my success. It is about always seeking God deeper.

Through the revolution in my own life, I have learned that much good and bad can be done in Jesus' name for The Ministry's* sake, God does not need The Ministry* for his will to be done on earth as it is in heaven. He chooses to need nothing more than empty hands—hands willing to receive from no one and nothing but him.

This is the Empty Hand Revolution. It starts and ends with every single person who has, is, or will walk the earth. It turns out, God's Kingdom cannot be taken or given, only received with empty hands.

To find out more, visit: http://www.emptyhandrevolution.com.

*The capital "M" ministry can be defined as the work we so benevolently do for God in contrast to the infinitely more important work God does for us.

A GREETING FROM THE AUTHOR

THANKS SO MUCH FOR reading *Empty Hand Revolution*. I hope I've successfully conveyed some fraction of the awe I felt while getting to know Cosmo Zimik and writing his story. He simply isn't the kind of guy you stumble across every day.

Within these pages, I have unapologetically recorded Cosmo's journey in a holistic manner, including his spirituality. Forward and back, up and down, Cosmo's life experiences have taught him to believe in a personal, creator God—one who has endeavored to teach Cosmo the lesson of the empty-handed revolution.

For those of you readers who adhere to a secular worldview (or a spiritual one other than Christianity), it is likely you've known "believers" who've remained equally as selfish and jerk-like after their conversion experience as before.

It's true, the journey or process of following Jesus the Christ often comes in fits and starts. For some followers, progress comes more slowly than others.

For Cosmo, the lesson of the empty hand revolution finally hit home in 2010 when he opened a dojo under the name Empty Hand Combat in downtown Nampa, Idaho. There, discarded and victimized children began to teach Cosmo as he labored to teach them.

From the jungles of northeast India to the bungalows of Nampa, Cosmo bore the negative effects of oppression and poverty. As a child, he vowed to take and protect what was his—for both himself and his people. Personal vows of such a nature are binding and difficult to overcome. In maintaining those vows, Cosmo performed both terrible and wonderful deeds.

In the broader culture, taking and being taken from are common ways of life for most of us on planet earth, secular and spiritual alike. Very few humans have the guts to disengage from this common practice, even after transitioning from takees to takers. Well known across the globe, and recorded in the annals of history, Mahatma Gandhi was one such courageous individual. He inspired much good during the formative years of India's republic.

Jesus was another odd individual who taught unlikely things such as "turning the other cheek" and "going the extra mile." He dared instruct an oppressed people group with outrageous concepts like "the meek shall inherit the earth" and "pray for those who persecute you."

The man was and is (for those who believe he still lives) offensive and unsettling to say the least. And yet, his teaching stands, despite its 2000 year-old status, naked and tempting for those few who find themselves inexplicably drawn to it like bugs to a zapper.

And what does that teaching say? For Cosmo Zimik it insisted he let go and stop grasping. In a world drunk on power that knows only violence, true greatness requires humility. Courage requires surrender. Developing into a warrior on such terms has been Cosmo's life quest—from Manipur to Delhi to Idaho.

But each individual must fight his or her own empty hand revolution —the inevitable personal war against whatever vows he or she may have made previously. The empty hand revolution is a war to let go of the things we can't do without, or so the script goes. Each of us has an impossible lesson to teach the world. In most cases, these are false lessons the world taught us.

Cosmo had convinced himself he needed to teach Delhi a lesson. He needed to teach Indians a lesson about the value and nobility of the Naga. In reality, he needed to let go of the false lesson soldiers had taught him at the age of four—that poor, tribal people are less than human.

Nine times out of ten, our grasping and fighting isn't teaching anyone anything, except to reinforce the lie. The empty hand revolution is an invitation to flip the script. Stop fighting for the lie. Empty your hands so you can receive the truth.

What that looks like is for each of us to discover. Perhaps it looks like cooking meals or picking up trash, teaching kids or providing a listening ear. Perhaps your truth revolves around self-image or social justice. Whatever it is, you won't find it all at once. Not even the best of us do.

As for me, my life certainly hasn't been as dramatic as Cosmo's. But I'll spend a page introducing myself nonetheless. After a classic eighties' childhood as a rancher's son in Texas, I attended University of Montana, then spent thirteen years as a campus pastor with InterVarsity Christian Fellowship at Boise State University and the University of Utah.

In 2009, my wife and I made the decision to jettison our lucrative day jobs, move, and raise a family while I pursued full time work as a novelist and writer. During the four-plus years since, we've been thrust into an empty hand revolution of our own. (It turns out writers don't make much money. Who knew?)

Two sons and eight books later, I found myself living in Nampa, Idaho and taking my eldest boy to kung fu classes at Empty Hand Combat. As I pieced together the events of Cosmo's life through impromptu stories he shared with his students, it struck me there was a book waiting to be written.

I offered my services. Why not, I thought. I've jumped off a series of cliffs already. What's one more?

A handful of months later, I'm still dangling in midair, unsure of what awaits below. Perhaps a move to Asia. Perhaps an unforeseen future as a social justice advocate through the written word. Perhaps a boost in my efforts to write exciting and challenging adventure stories for young and old alike. Or maybe a future as a ghost chili farmer.

Thus goes the empty hand revolution and the life of its revolutionaries. Never dull, never certain beyond what is certain.

If you find yourself in the market for a good novel, something along the adventure, science fiction, dystopian or sci-fi thriller genres, here is a list of my works to date:

The DMB Files
De Novo Syndrome (#1)
Desert Gods (#2)

Relic Hunters
First Relic (#1)

The Green Ones
Written and Published weekly @www.epifiction.com, coming in 2014/15

All *Lost DMB Files* allowing for suspected gaps
Reefer Ranger (#9)
Del Rio Con Amor (#14)
Fistful of Reefer (#17)
The Austin Job (#18)
Hell's Womb (#22)
Get Doc Quick (#24)
McCutchen's Bones (#25)
Twitch and Die! (#26)
Paraplegic Zombie Slayer (#35)
Fourth Horseman (#43)

Immediately after this greeting I've also included a teaser for my upcoming adventure series, *Cosmo and Chancho*. Based on a purely fictional pairing of a young Cosmo and an equally enterprising orphan from Mexico named Chancho, the *Cosmo and Chancho* series strikes an interesting balance between *Indiana Jones*, *Tomb Raider* and *The Adventures of Tin Tin*.

Feel free to stalk me via, http://davidmarkbrownwrites.com as well as at http://www.emptyhandrevolution.com. Above all, enjoy the show!

APPENDICES

Teaser for Cosmo and Chancho

A LINE OF DARK-skinned Africans zig-zagged out of sight behind mountains of bituminous coal. Coaling a behemoth the size of the Royal Edward was a monumental and dirty task. Cosmo gathered a bird's eye view of the process from his favorite spot on the aft deck of the five-level passenger steamer.

Shielding his face with his hand, Cosmo peered upward at the sun through the slits between his fingers. The temperature and humidity combined to create an oppressive heat as bad as anything he had grown up with in the jungles of Northeast India. The workers' only protection against the sun were the baskets of coal perched on their heads.

Sweat streaked down the laborers dust-covered faces as they marched steadily forward. One basket-full at a time, they dumped the precious coal into the ship's hopper. After an hour, the snaking line of workers continued with no end in sight.

Watching the coal porters renewed Cosmo's gratitude for his current job as bodyguard to the less than noble Sir Rendel Wrightwick. Technically, Cosmo's title was porter and baggage boy. One of Wrightwick's colleagues had jokingly referred to him as an esquire.

After sneaking a peek at his boss's English/Hindi dictionary, Cosmo had learned an esquire had once been the title for a knight in training. He liked it. *Cosmo Zimik, Esquire.*

"Cosmo?"

Without acknowledging the voice, Cosmo attempted to identify it.

"Is that you?"

By the accent Cosmo could tell the voice belonged to a white man, American. That could mean only one thing—a missionary. Cosmo faced him.

"I wouldn't of believed it, but Laura insisted it was you."

Cosmo recognized the man, but couldn't recall the name. "Pastor…"

"Pettigrew."

Cosmo nodded. The Baptist missionary and his wife had been working throughout the Naga Hills for several years. Cosmo had met them during his father's ordination. What were the chances someone connected with his home village would end up on the Royal Edward? The last thing he needed was for his father to learn he had left his Calcutta boarding school.

Pettigrew frowned. "What are you doing out here in the middle of the Arabian Sea?"

Cosmo turned the tables with a question of his own. "Are you and your wife heading home on sabbatical?"

Pettigrew raised his hat long enough to run his fingers through his hair. "A bit of a fundraising junket, I'm afraid. We hope to travel back to India soon. It's only been a week, and I miss your Naga Hills already. But enough about me and Laura."

Cosmo dodged the matter. "I miss home too. You must be looking forward to seeing your home in the States."

"Well yes, I suppose Virginia will always be home. But for heaven's sake, you must tell me how you've ended up—"

"You there! Bag boy."

Cosmo blinked slowly and faced Wrightwick's personal assistant, Barnard. He was an overly scrupulous and annoying man in general. Currently, his appearance served as a welcome interruption.

"Stop your lolly-gagging, you goldbricker. The boss has a meeting in Aden in fifteen minutes. You've got fifteen seconds to meet him on the dock, or start swimming back to India." Barnard glared through his circular spectacles at Pettigrew.

Apparently, Cosmo didn't need to introduce the two men.

Pettigrew sputtered before finding his tongue. "You're working for Sir Wrightwick?"

Cosmo had no idea how an American Baptist missionary knew of a disreputable business man like Wrightwick, but the unfortunate coincidences were adding up. Instead of answering the question, Cosmo leapt on top of the railing.

Pettigrew gasped. "What would your father think?"

Nearly three feet over Cosmo's head, a guy wire tethered the Royal Edward to a concrete anchor amidst the coal piles. Cosmo glanced down at Barnard. "Can I borrow a kerchief?"

Barnard scoffed. "A kerchief? Boy, you'd better be worried more about your hide than a runny nose." Despite his grumbling, Barnard fetched the cloth from his pocket. Reaching up, he slapped it into Cosmo's outstretched hand. "Now you've got ten seconds, so I suggest you get down and stop—"

Cosmo doubled the cloth in his hand, bent his knees and jumped. With an inch to spare, he clutched the cable, which turned out to be as big around as a five rupee coin. The kerchief smoked in Cosmo's hand as he zipped down the steep angle—perhaps too steep.

Imagining the flesh of his hand smoking next, Cosmo scanned for a safe place to land. Heat seared the palm of his hand. Swinging toward a less trafficked stretch of boardwalk, Cosmo released his grip and plummeted the last several yards to the dock. Despite tucking his feet on contact, his knees struck his chest harder than he would have liked.

After tumbling into a shocked laborer, Cosmo stood with a stupid grin on his face. "Nine seconds to spare." He spoke to no one in particular.

Pettigrew called a parting shot after him. "It would kill your father to find out how you're using your skills!"

Cosmo ground his teeth and pushed through the snaking line of coal porters. Hundreds of miles from India, and his father's watchful eye still pursued him. Cosmo would simply have to travel further. He didn't expect his father or any of his people to understand why he'd taken a job protecting a representative of Colonial Britain.

Then again, as an American and a missionary, of course Pettigrew had been referring to Cosmo's neglect of his spiritual gifting. Of all the stupid things his father could have handed down to his youngest son...Cosmo shook it off. Somehow, he would have to avoid Pettigrew for the remainder of their time aboard the Royal Edward.

Covered in coal dust and several seconds late, Cosmo finally located his boss. Lateness and untidiness were two things Wrightwick typically did not tolerate in his associates or employees. For some reason, Cosmo's contempt for his boss exempted him from severe punishment.

Currently, Sir Wrightwick looked undecided between rage and amusement. "The landing could have been better." He sucked the toothpick in his teeth before flicking it off the dock and into the water below.

Cosmo nodded. "I'll work on it. No problem."

***

The settlement of Aden existed for one purpose, the coaling of ships. Decades earlier, a Sultanate of Yemen had surrendered the volcanic spit to the British East India Company and a battalion of Royal Marines. Built inside an extinct volcano, the town was perfectly sheltered against storms and pirates alike. Unfortunately, the walls of dark, igneous rock protected the town from any and all breeze as well.

On full alert, Cosmo rode shotgun next to the coach's driver. After a series of switchbacks, the horse-drawn carriage arrived at the local's version of a house of spirits. Cosmo had no use for alcohol or any adult who imbibed it. His people, the Naga, didn't touch the stuff. From what Cosmo could tell, they had good reason.

While Wrightwick didn't drink excessively, his business appointments usually convened in such places. Cosmo jumped down and opened the door of the carriage for his boss.

Wrightwick flushed from the carriage like a flock of birds from the jungle canopy. Always in a hurry without looking hurried, that was Wrightwick's manner. As a result, the man came across as angry and intimidating. He knew what he wanted, and he expected others to keep up.

Usually Cosmo's young age forced him to work twice as hard to overcome initial impressions. But Wrightwick had seemed pleased by Cosmo's youth. He had recognized Cosmo's abilities immediately and hired him after a fifteen minute interview during which Cosmo revealed next to nothing about himself personally.

Handing Cosmo his satchel, Wrightwick flung open the saloon doors. He paused long enough for his eyes to adjust to the dim lighting.

Cosmo flowed past Wrightwick without brushing his elbow. He sized up every individual inside the drinking house in a matter of seconds. By the time Wrightwick proceeded to a table in the far corner, Cosmo had eliminated all but two of the patrons as potential threats.

Cosmo followed his boss while keeping one eye glued on the backs of the two burley fellows seated at the bar. Cosmo didn't like the fact that their turbans and flowing robes could conceal swords or even rifles.

"Sir Wrightwick, I presume." A portly gentlemen rose from the corner table.

Wrightwick sat without shaking the man's hand. "I've no time for such unscheduled diversions. You have information for me, Mr. Crampton?"

Crampton attempted to brush his hair from his face. Excessive sweating had pasted it to his forehead. The man was nervous, slovenly and alone. He lacked the confidence to pose any serious threat.

Cosmo turned his back to the meeting. Tensing, he realized the two men at the bar had gone. He swept the establishment with his eyes. How could such men disappear so quickly and so quietly? At the very least, Cosmo should have heard them upsetting a chair or a table.

"Right you are." Crampton worked up the nerve to speak. "Terribly sorry for the interruption."

"Then get to it, man." Wrightwick snapped.

Cosmo observed the remaining patrons for clues to the mystery mens' disappearance. None of them stared toward the exit or acted as if anything strange had occurred. Cosmo knew he had turned his head for only a second.

"Right, right." Crampton stammered. "A scurrilous lot filtered through here the better of two days ago asking after the Royal Edward in a round about manner, if you know what I mean."

"Similar to your current manner?" Wrightwick asked through clenched teeth.

"I see. Indeed, you're right." Crampton gulped. "Straight to the point then. There's no doubt in my mind they were pirates, sir. Mercenaries hired with the specific charge of finding your ship."

Cosmo didn't like the mention of pirates, especially after losing the two men at the bar. He reasoned the men could have been waiting for Wrightwick's arrival before setting some devious plot into action.

"Mercenaries and pirates. Hmmm." Wrightwick scratched his chin. "I apologize for my brash behavior, Mr. Crampton. You were right for initiating this aside. You've provided useful information indeed. It's possible the Ottoman Empire has caught wind of our movements in the area."

While maintaining his vigilance, Cosmo focused on the conversation. He'd undertaken a crash course on Middle Eastern current events after learning of the Royal Edward's destination. An English newspaper had revealed the Ottomans were currently engaged in a localized war with neighboring countries. Cosmo surmised on his own that Wrightwick's interest in the area pivoted on the warfare.

"Think closely, Mr. Crampton." Wrightwick leaned forward. "Did these dastards pronounce the name of the Royal Edward specifically?"

Crampton shook his head. "Nay, sir. But they inquired after large steamers en route to the Suez Canal. You know, asking whether one had been by. Only three boats this week fit that description."

"Indeed, the coincidence is suspicious. I agree."

Both men fell silent. A wooden chair scraped the floorboards as a patron rose to pay his bill. Cosmo wondered again of the mystery men, then dismissed them as paranoia. Coincidence. Probably nothing. The alien environment had set Cosmo on edge.

Crampton cleared his voice. "Should I inform her Majesty of any changes in the plan?"

"No no." Wrightwick stood. This time he extended his hand.

Crampton shook it.

"Everything will proceed as planned. I'll double the watch, that's all. Nothing will prevent the Edward from landing intact with its cargo. Certainly no band of clumsy pirates." Wrightwick glanced at the timepiece on his wrist and gestured for Cosmo to take the lead.

With his boss's satchel still in hand, Cosmo moved swiftly toward the exit. If Wrightwick was deferring to Cosmo's lead, it meant he was concerned enough for his safety to throw convention out the window. Not that anyone in the saloon would care that a British gentleman had deferred to his bag boy. But Cosmo knew Wrightwick cared.

That meant Cosmo should care. Throwing open the saloon doors, Cosmo leapt aside and held one open for his boss. He blinked rapidly in the harsh midday sun. Two blurs in the shapes of men flashed to his left.

Cosmo shielded the sun with his free hand. His bleary eyes focused on an empty street. No men, no nothing. He whistled for the carriage parked across the way. The horses pawed at the ground. The driver started as if he'd been asleep beneath the brim of his hat. Straightening, he shook the reins and stirred the horses to life.

Cosmo opened the door of the carriage. After Wrightwick boarded, Cosmo resumed shotgun. He rubbed his eyes and scanned both sides of the street for the mysterious men or anything suspicious. A couple of women shrouded in black burkas emerged from a bakery. They scurried from the presence of the strangers immediately.

Maybe he wasn't getting enough sleep. Due to the heightened threat, he'd be getting less in the next few days. Cosmo was determined to execute his duty with honor.

Before ditching boarding school, Cosmo had been exposed to

Sun Tzu's *Art of War* and the imperative to "know your enemy." Thus, Cosmo's motivations in protecting the corrupt and dishonorable Sir Wrightwick might be less than pure. Still, he took the contract seriously.

There was no reason Cosmo couldn't study his enemy while maintaining his honor. Besides, if pirates were targeting the Royal Edward, everyone onboard would be in equal danger. Cosmo included…

END OF TEASER

*To find out more about Cosmo and Chancho, visit: http://davidmarkbrownwrites.com or http://www.emptyhandrevolution.com.

Naga Resources

THE SILENCING OF YOUTH

Based on the events surrounding "Operation Bluebird" in the Oinam Hills, *The Silencing of Youth* is an essay recorded by the Universal Periodic Review of the United Nations. It attempts to summarize the events at Oinam and the 72-page report written by Amnesty International.

PRESS RELEASE: Amsterdam, January 5th, 2013

Cost of the Indo-Naga War Estimated: Part One, Human Cost

The Government of India (GOI) has neither released official nor unofficial figures of the human cost of the six-decades-old war it unleashed on Nagaland in 1954. Practically unknown internationally, this long-running war (possibly the longest of modern times) has Indian journalists repeating, one after the other, a death toll of 25,000.

Without mentioning the much larger number of casualties on either side, the GOI and media completely disregard the figure of 300,000 dead Nagas, as recorded by the Naga Peoples Movement for Human Rights (NPMHR). This astounding number does nothing to include an injury count of the Armed Forces of India.

The disparity between the inclusive 25,000 death toll provided by GOI and the 300,000 dead Nagas according to HPMHR suggest a lack of transparency at the very least. Consequently for the GOI, questions like this unfold:

- What is the reason for the Government of India to withhold these figures?

- What is their reason to withhold deaths and casualties of the Armed Forces of India?

Even though peace talks between India and Nagaland have been ongoing since 1997 (with no tangible result), the secrecy around the overwhelming human cost of this war should be known, if only because India is a Democratic Nation and therefore accountable to its people.

This is so, not only with respect to the tremendous number of deaths on both sides, but also with respect to the yet unknown but surely larger number of soldiers and civilians who were injured, tortured, maimed and invalidated (unable to work).

Hence the Naga International Support Center urges the international community to broker peace between India and Nagaland, thus mediating an ending this seemingly endless war, by:

- Sending a fact-finding mission to factually determine the human cost of the Indo/Naga War
- Presenting the results to the United Nations, the Indian Government, and to the National and International Media
- Mapping out and establishing the amount of casualties of this war on both sides, publishing the results internationally, and demanding accountability

For more information visit www.nagalim.nl (website of Naga International Support Center).

PRESS RELEASE: Amsterdam, January 5th, 2013:
Cost of the Indo-Naga War Estimated: Part Two, Money
Cost of Indo-Naga War amounts to $23,368,333,334 USD

To date, the Government of India, (GOI) has not released official figures about the war it unleashed on the Naga peoples in 1954. Since then, neither the rationale for starting nor perpetuating the war have been made public record. The GOI has no publicly-stated policy in regards to ending it.

This means the Indian electorate has no official means of knowing anything about the Indo-Naga war. Absence of policies also means the Government of India cannot be held accountable for the loss of life or the exorbitant sums of taxpayers' money spent on the endless war.

Due to the acknowledged sovereignty of India, the international community judged the Indo-Naga War a domestic war. The Naga International Support Center (NISC) holds the United Nations responsible for not honoring the Naga Declaration of Independence it received in 1947, which in turn, motivated India to forcibly incorporate the Naga Nation.

The following conservatively calculated financial cost of the Indo-Naga war reveals what the GOI did in name of the Indian public without informing them, and thus depriving them of the democratic means of holding the GOI in check.

Estimated over 60 years:

Salaries: 200,000 Indian Army soldiers and paramilitary at 6,000 Rupees per head per month, calculated over 60 years: 6,000 x 200,000 x 12 months x 60 years=

864,000,000,000 Rupees

Food: 200,000 x 60 rupees per day = 12,000,000 x 365 days x 60 years=

262,800,000,000 Rupees

Housing infrastructure: Barracks in many villages as well as stockades and camps, head and other military quarters estimated 1,500 x 5,000,000 = 75,000,000,000

Maintenance 1,500 x 2,000,000 = 3,000,000,000 + 75,000,000,000=

78,000,000,000 Rupees

Mobility: trucks, tanks, assault vehicles, cars: 5,000 x 5,000,000 = 20,500,000,000

fuel of 1,000,000 liters a year at 80 rupees a liter = 60 x 80.000.000 = 4,800,000,000

25,300,000,000 Rupees

Weaponry in dollars: 200,000 rifles at $100 USD x 10 for replacements = 200,000 x 10 x $100 USD=

$200.000.000 USD

Total amount of unaccounted monies:
1,390,100,000,000 Rupees + $200,000,000 USD=
$23,368,333,334 USD

We did not include allowances paid to soldiers for serving in dangerous areas, for duty in mountains etc.. Also not taken into account were big weapons such as machine guns, cannons, howitzers, patriots, airplanes, bombs, fighter jets, etc.

With this conservatively calculated estimate, the Naga International Support Center wishes to inspire (even dare) the Indian press, international press, political organizations and/or parties, and research institutes to investigate the actual cost of war so the Indian people will know how their money has been (as is being) spent.

The home website for the Naga International Support Center can be found here:

http://www.nagalim.nl/

For further reading:

Forbidden Land: Quest for Nagalim by Frans Welman

Out of Isolation: Exploring a Forgotten World by Frans Welman

Naga Harvest Festival by Frans Welman

Nagaland Chronicle: Over the Hills and Down the Valleys by George Kurian

Knowing Jesus: The Big Story

THE FOLLOWING IS ADAPTED from *True Story* by James Choung. Copyright (c) 2008 by James Choung. Used by permission of InterVarsity Press, P.O. Box 1400, Downers Grove, IL 60515, USA. www.ivpress.com. It represents the core message Jesus came to teach.

What's our world like? What do you see on the news?

Most people would agree that our world is pretty messed up. But what is more interesting is the human response, or how one feels about the world one lives in. No normal person thinks suffering, violence and oppression are good things.

So what does this mean?

Most people ache for a better world. But our universal ache speaks of something more. Just like hunger points to food and thirst points to water, so our universal ache for a better world means that such a world either once existed or will one day exist.

Part I: Designed for Good

In the Christian worldview, God created a good, wonderful world. In the beginning, everything was right with each other.

On a bigger level, creation was designed to take care of us and we were designed to take care of creation. We were made to be interdependent on each other.

On a relational level, people were designed to take care of each other. They were made to be in true community, with the freedom to love and be loved, to serve and be served, to be themselves without shame in front of each other.

Lastly, on a personal level, we were each designed to be in a relationship with the God, one full of love and intimacy. God hung out with us, and we liked being with him. We were meant to love and serve each other as well. (The inner circle to represent God's presence with us.)

The world and all that's in it was designed for good.

But what happened to this good world? How did we get to where we are today?

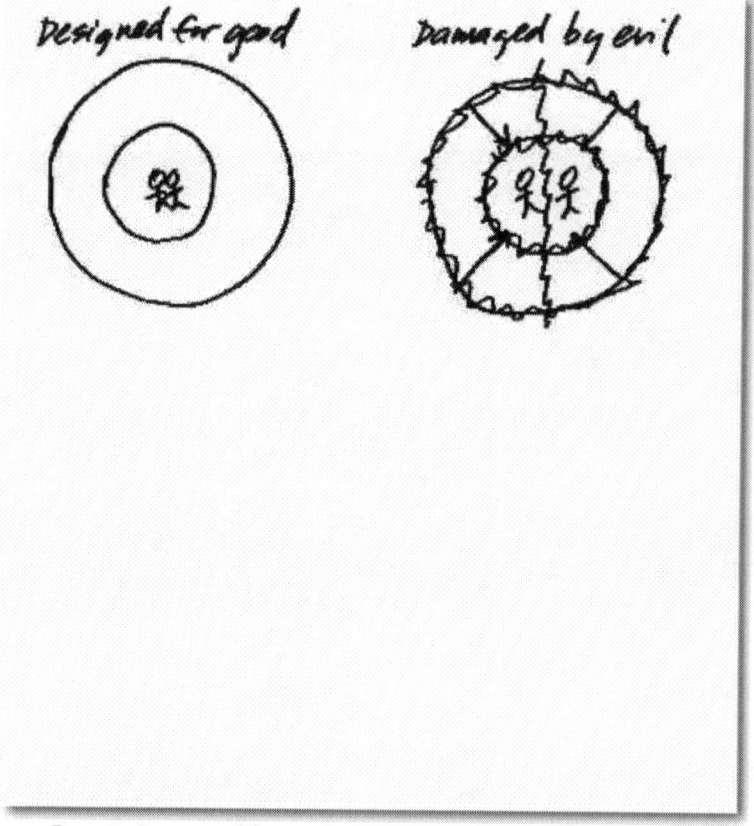

Part 2: Damaged by Evil

When God was in charge, we had a wonderful world. But we wanted to be in charge so that all of creation and everyone in it could be used for our own benefit instead of its intended design and purpose to serve each other. It became all about us.

On the bigger level, we damaged creation. We drain her for her oil, and fill the air with pollutants so we can have a comfortable lifestyle. And it fights back in hurricanes and tsunamis. But there are also other larger issues, such as racism, sexism, slavery, corruption, injustice and oppression that damages us and our world.

On a relational level, we damage each other and others hurt us—whether we mean to or not. When we live for only ourselves, then it's easy to take and gain without regard for other people.

And on a personal level, we damage our soul and its relationship with God. We are afraid of God now, and in our fear, we try to ignore him and live for ourselves. But we are only hurting ourselves, and we will never be the kinds of people that we want and dream to be.

We, and the world, are damaged by evil. We're all damaged, and are consistently contributing to the mess.

Where have you seen damage in your own life or the lives around you?

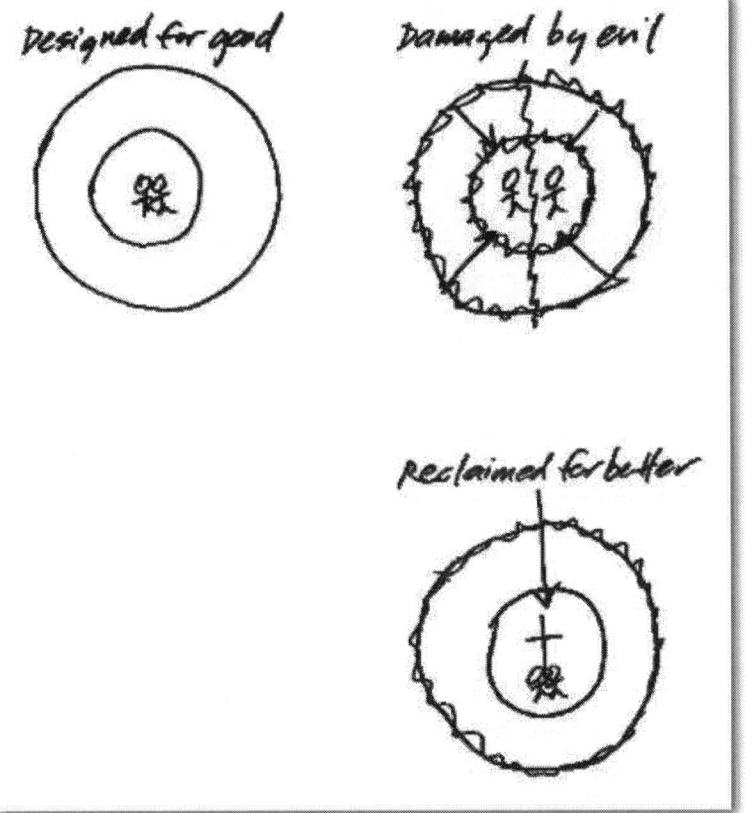

Part 3: Restored for Better

But God loved the world too much to leave it this way.

God came to the planet as Jesus 2,000 years ago and started a new thing. He started a resistance movement against evil, though not with military revolt, or communal escapism. Instead, he taught us a better way to live, and wants to give us the power to overcome evil in us and around us.

Jesus took on all of the damage and died on the cross, letting it die with him. But he also came back to life, proving that evil doesn't have the final word. And in the mystery of faith, we too die with Jesus to truly live in and with him. In so doing, everything, including us, is all restored for better.

On a bigger level, he restored creation so that all of it could be used in their good ways. All of the world's systems " the environment, corporations, governments, schools, etc. " can now be used to usher in God's values of love, peace and justice. Oppression and injustice can cease.

He also restored our relationships, so that we can love and forgive each other. Damaged relationships can be healed.

Lastly, God restored our relationships with himself. People don't have to live self-centered lives or be afraid of God anymore. He forgives the ways we contribute to the damage in the world. Now we can truly live with God, in a relationship full of love and intimacy.

The good news: the revolution has begun, and we're all invited. **Jesus came to restore the world and everything in it for better.**

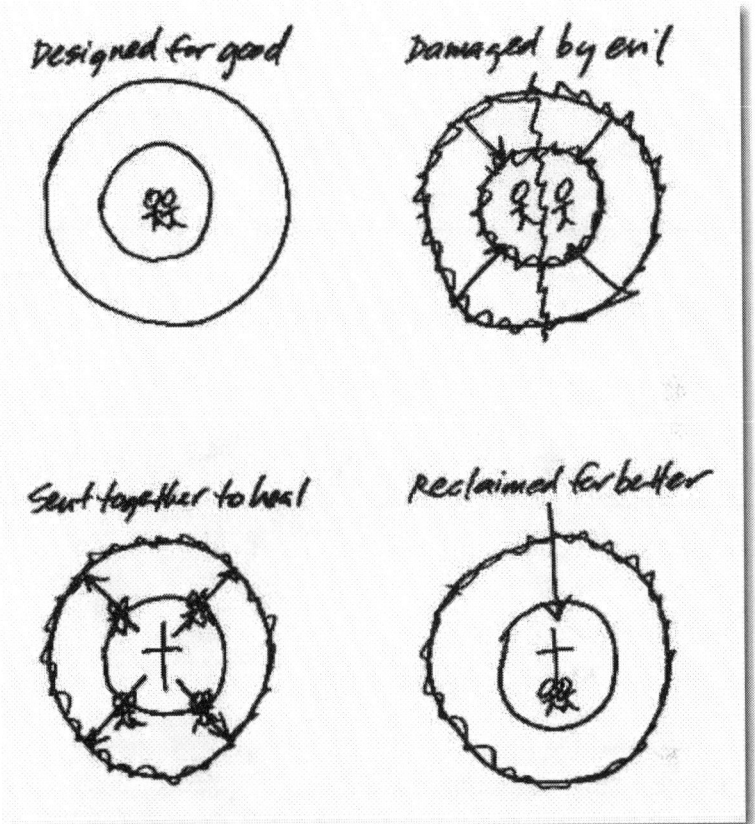

Part 4: Sent Together to Heal

Jesus wants us to join this resistance movement against evil, to go out and heal the world.

On a personal level, we're called to submit to Jesus' leadership and become more like him. We need to become the kind of good we want to see in the world. So we admit our contribution to the damage, and trust Jesus, letting him take charge of our lives instead. (The inner circle represents God's presence.)

As we're becoming more like Jesus, we're also called to heal relationships, our own and others. We ask for forgiveness, and forgive others. Then we're freed to love each other.

Lastly, on a bigger level, we're called to heal systems. We're called to protect and heal the environment. We're called to fight injustice and oppression. It's overwhelming, but we're called to do it together. (The arrows leading outward represent God's Spirit.)

Many Christians around us have gotten stuck in the third circle, not helping to heal the planet. But Jesus wanted his followers to be in this fourth circle, by being sent together to heal.

We don't go alone, but with the power of God's Spirit and the community of God's people with us. He'll be with us. **With these resources, Jesus is asking us to be sent together to heal the planet.**

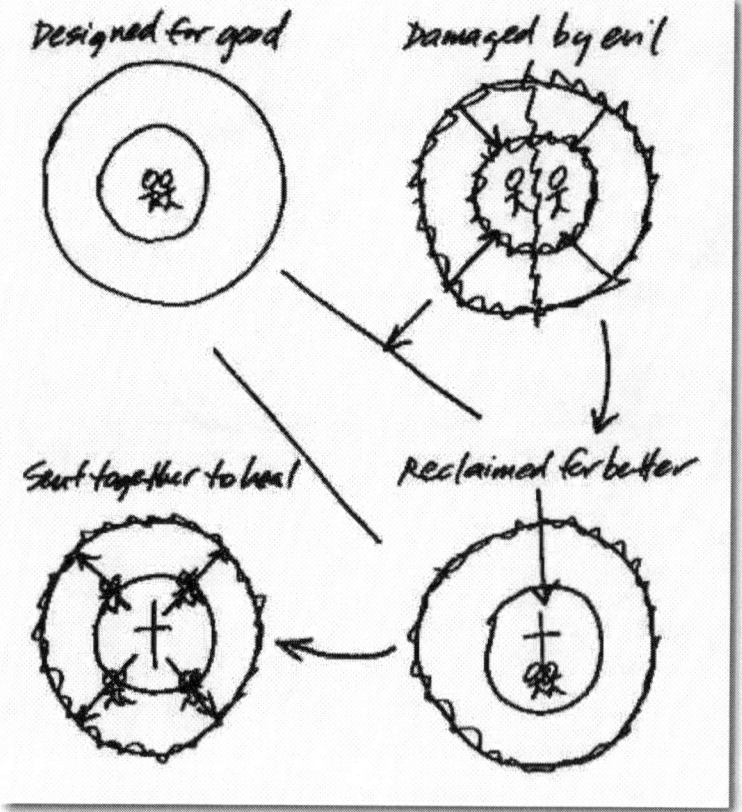

Response

We can't go straight to the last circle. **We need to become the kind of good we want to see in the world.** In everything we do, we bring all that we are—our motivations, our instincts, our methods, etc. We are all damaged too, and we need healing before we can heal the world around us. Jesus does that the best. By trusting him, and giving him leadership over our lives, we can become the kind of good we want to see around us.

So, which one of these circles do you relate to? In the first, everything's fine. In the second, you're overwhelmed by the problems. In the third, you've made some commitment to Jesus but are holding back. In the fourth, you're in the movement of God with his people. Where are you?

- If you're in the first, you've probably already acknowledged the world needs help. What's your role in helping to heal the world?
- If you're in the second circle, find a Christian friend to talk to about it. (If you don't know anyone, contact David Mark Brown via his website, http://www.davidmarkbrownwrites.com) Jesus is offering you a way to overcome. Would you like to know how?
- If you're in the third circle, that's a great start. But it's clear that Jesus is asking you for more. What's keeping you from joining his movement to heal the world?
- If you're in the fourth circle, what you're doing is in line with the values of the Kingdom of God, but you could be doing so much more with God's presence and with his people. You could be a part of something that will last. Would you like to be a part of it? Would you like to let Jesus be the leader of your life and join his movement to heal the planet? Will you trust him with your life? (Thus joining the Empty Hand Revolution.)
- If you're making a decision toward Jesus, that's awesome! Jesus also wants to give you resources for this mission, such as the Holy Spirit and the Bible. Find someone to share your decision with—someone who can pray with you and help you along the journey.

Frequently Asked Questions

1.) Didn't Jesus die for our sins? Is the other stuff really a part of the Gospel?

Jesus died for our sins. Absolutely. But does that mean he merely died for the penalty of our sins? If he died for only the penalty, then we don't have to change. But he also died for our sin itself, then the power of sin is also truly dead in us. We are saved and delivered from our sin, and thus can change. We can finally become the people of God we were meant to be.

Also, looking at Colossians 1:20, it's clear that Jesus didn't just come to save individuals, but "to reconcile to himself all things, whether things on earth or things in heaven, by making peace through his blood, shed on the cross." That includes not only us, but also our relationships and the systems around us " all things. This diagram is just an attempt of putting the Gospel back in its original context.

2.) Is this really the Gospel? If this is Biblical, why haven't people taught this in our churches?

Nothing in the diagram is new. If it's new, it's probably heretical. But all of this old truth is often locked behind the Bible's many pages or in theological tomes, and so seems inaccessible to the normal Christian. So the teaching has been around, but we need something simpler so that Jesus' central message can be recaptured more broadly.

3.) So then, what actually happens with Jesus' Crucifixion and Resurrection?

Many Biblical metaphors of atonement exist. One of the earliest is the ransom view by Origen. Satan held humankind hostage, but God tricked Satan into accepting Jesus as a ransom. Satan accepted, thus freeing mankind, but lost again because death couldn't hold Jesus. In the moral influence theory, 11th century scholar Pierre Abélard argued that Jesus is the great example of service and sacrifice in devotion to God, which culminates in the Cross. His example changes us to be selfless. In the Christus Victor theory, Jesus takes on all of the evil and damage of the planet onto himself and it all dies with him. But it doesn't hold him back. Instead he comes back to life, he brings new life into all of these old structures and people. He faces and overcomes death, and we are free from sin, death and the Devil. The penal substitution theory we know arose in the 11th century by Anselm, but was codified in the 13th century by Thomas Aquinas and then applied to individuals by John Calvin in the 16th century. They all help explain the Big Story.

In it all, our invitation is to participate in his death and resurrection each day " to carry our cross daily " in a communal and world context. In this way, we die in Christ and live in Christ each day.

4.) What if someone just wants to jump to the fourth circle, and ignore the third? Why do we need Jesus to heal the planet?

Ultimately, we need to become the kind of good that we want to see in the world.

Besides, it's the stuff that will last. Think about every beneficial major social revolution out there in the past two thousand years: public education, health care, human rights, children's rights, women's suffrage, civil rights, literacy education, rights for the disabled " even fair-trade coffee " and more were all started by Christians. The only major movement I could think of that didn't seem to have Christian beginnings are non-violent resistance movements, which could mark their beginnings with Gandhi. But he admits that he learned it from the Gospels of Jesus! The followers of Jesus have a good track record of leaving behind the kind of good that lasts.

To be fair, there were the Inquisitions, Crusades, and Western Imperialism. Yes, these were atrocities, and Jesus' name was smeared. But think of major irreligious movements of our time. Communism alone claimed 100 million lives, far more than the Inquisitions or the Crusades combined. I'm just trying to balance things out.

5.) Can you recommend some books that will go deeper into the themes of this diagram?

A good, basic primer is Allen Wakabayashi's *Kingdom Come*. *The Divine Conspiracy* by Dallas Willard can help you go deeper. For atonement metaphors, Scot McKnight's *A Community Called Atonement* is helpful. And to learn more about Jesus in his cultural context, go with N. T. Wright's *The Challenge of Jesus*. And his *Simply Christian* is one of the best books explaining the faith to a postmodern world.

Bible Verses Referenced During The Big Story

Genesis 1:29-30, 2:15
Genesis 2:25
Genesis 3:9
Genesis 3:14-19; Ezekiel 16:49; Amos 5:4-15; Ephesians 6:12
Genesis 3:12-13; Romans 1:18-32
Genesis 3:10; Romans 1:18-32
2 Corinthians 5:21
Philippians 1:21; Luke 9:23
Ephesians 2:11-22; Colossians 1:15-20
Matthew 6:12, 18:21-35
2 Corinthians 5:11-21; Colossians 3:1-17
Romans 6:23; 2 Corinthians 5:17; Colossians 3:1-17; 1 John 1:9
Matthew 6:12, 18:21-35; 2 Corinthians 5:11-21
Genesis 2:15; Exodus 23:1-13; Leviticus 19:9-15, 23:22, 25:1-54; Deuteronomy 15:1-18; Ezekiel 16:49
Isaiah 41:10; Matthew 28:20

Made in the USA
Charleston, SC
25 July 2014